OUR CULTURE:

ITS CHRISTIAN ROOTS AND PRESENT CRISIS

OUR CULTURE:

ITS CHRISTIAN ROOTS AND PRESENT CRISIS

Edward Alleyn Lectures 1944

Edited by

V. A. DEMANT, D.Litt.

Canon and Chancellor of St. Paul's

WIPF & STOCK · Eugene, Oregon

Wipf and Stock Publishers
199 W 8th Ave, Suite 3
Eugene, OR 97401

Our Culture
Its Christian Roots and Present Crisis
By Demant, V. A. and Hodges, H. A.
Copyright©1947 SPCK
ISBN 13: 978-1-5326-1419-4
Publication date 10/26/2017
Previously published by SPCK, 1947

PREFACE

THE following lectures were delivered in Christ's Chapel of Alleyn's College of God's Gift at Dulwich, on Friday evenings during the summer term of 1944 and the winter term of 1945. The Rev. C. W. Dugmore, B.D., then Chaplain of the College, had approached me with the request that I should arrange a course of lectures to follow the series given on the same foundation in 1943. That series, on *The Interpretation of the Bible*, was edited by Mr. Dugmore and published by S.P.C.K. in 1944. Mr. Dugmore's preface to that volume explains fully the character and history of the Foundation. It is due to his initiative and to the ready response of the College governors to it, that two series of 'Edward Alleyn Lectures' have been undertaken and carried out.

The subject chosen for 1944 was suggested by the need for clarifying the widespread feeling that our modern civilization is in a critical condition, and that this condition has something to do with what has happened to the religious forces which have helped to mould our Western European culture.

The lecturers who have collaborated with me in carrying out this programme deserve a special word of gratitude over and above that due to them for putting their knowledge and insight at the disposal of the lectureship. The lectures were delivered in the period of the flying-bomb attacks upon London in which Dulwich suffered very heavily. One or two lectures were interrupted by near-by explosions while speaker and audience took refuge under the seats. Before the course was completed the Chaplain lost his house and the College was so seriously damaged that the later lectures had to be postponed for six months.   On Mr. Dugmore's resignation the local arrangements for these postponed lectures were carried out magnificently by the Rev. H. H Dixon of Dulwich College.

V. A. DEMANT.

St. Paul's,
    London.
May, 1946.

CONTENTS

PAGE

PREFACE v
   By the Editor.

I. THE AIMS AND ASSUMPTIONS OF OUR CULTURE . 1
   By the Rev. V. A. Demant, D.Litt., Editor.

II. OUR CULTURE: ITS THOUGHT 17
   By H. A. Hodges, M.A., D.Phil., Professor of
   Philosophy in the University of Reading.

III. THE CRISIS OF CHRISTIAN CULTURE: EDUCATION . 35
   By Christopher Dawson, M.A.

IV. TOWARDS A CHRISTIAN AESTHETIC . . . 50
   By Dorothy L. Sayers, M.A.

V. WORK AND THE CRISIS OF OUR CULTURE . . 70
   By Maurice B. Reckitt, M.A., Editor of
   Christendom.

VI. OUR CULTURE: ITS RELIGION 97
   By the Rev. V. A. Demant, D.Litt., Editor.

I. THE AIMS AND ASSUMPTIONS OF OUR CULTURE

by

V. A. DEMANT

THE purpose of these lectures is to gain some insight into the Christian Religion by examining what has been its influence upon our culture, what is happening to our culture to-day, and what is required if the positive gains of that culture are to be preserved and developed.

Following lectures will deal with specific parts of that culture. I am to outline the question in this opening lecture. The word "culture" in this context is used in the sense in which the anthropologist uses it, to describe a certain pattern of life which influences the aims and habits of men. As we might speak of the culture of the Hebrides, or as W. H. Rivers wrote of the culture of Melanesia, so we speak of the culture of the European West to describe a set of outlooks, aims and ways of life, which has a history in the past of Europe and has spread to other parts of the world. Culture in this wider meaning includes the activities known as cultural in the narrower sense: the arts, sciences and education of a community—those which adorn and enrich life, and do not merely preserve or increase it. It comprises also the unofficial societies and associations which exist for some interest in which men may engage, but which are not vital to their physical and political existence. Those of you who attend these lectures are engaged in a cultural activity in the narrower sense. But in the wider meaning in which we are using the word in these lectures, the culture of a people or groups of people is concerned with the relation of all its functions: its organized activities in culture (in the narrower meaning), its politics, economic life and the naturally given forms of community like the family, as well as the free associations of those who are bound by social allegiances such as religion. Now, this whole pattern of life, which has a definite character, is very near to what we call civilization. It is the inner side of civilization. But civilization includes also the outward instruments and organization of a culture, like the machine-dominated civilization of our era, the commercial aim of our Anglo-Saxon conception of economic purpose, the peculiar power of the modern State over all other social groupings and activities. All that is part of our civilization. We are concerned with what is happening to it—what is good and bad in it or in the truly human interest. And so we are to look at its inner side: the aims, assumptions and habitual modes of life which have given rise to it, that inner side which I have called our culture.

Now, we are all inclined to think that a pattern of life we live in and approve of is something natural; that it is just part of the nature of things. Unless it is thwarted or opposed by peculiar perversity we think it is the kind of life-pattern all men would naturally attain to. This is the greatest of all mistakes. If the mistake continues to mislead us, then what is of value in European culture may well be lost to the human race for good.

To call a pattern of life a culture means two things: first, that the pattern is a historic growth; it depends upon certain definite influences in a historic period; if these influences cease to operate, the plants will continue to bloom like flowers in a vase for a time, but cut off from their roots they will not survive; secondly, to use the word "culture" for a life-pattern implies that it is something which requires tending—like a garden and the land. Man has a responsibility towards it; if he treats it as a wild forest that will continue to grow by itself it is doomed, and man with it. That is largely what has happened. We have taken our civilization for granted; or, to

change the metaphor, it has become an artificial super-
structure upon crumbling foundations; then the super-
structure has to be stuck up more firmly by something called
planning.

This culture which we inherit from past ages in Europe,
and which has its own variations of character in different
lands, as it has in our Anglo-Saxon culture, is in the twentieth
century the subject of a number of colossal revolutions. It is
in a state of crisis or judgment. This crisis, as I interpret it,
has two phases. In the "democratic" communities the aims
of men are on the whole still those of European civilization,
so largely formed by Christian outlooks; but the assumptions,
the things they take for granted and the habits considered
normal, have been formed by influences which are opposed to
the aims. This contradiction is not conscious. In the totalitarian countries, on the other hand, the conflict has been solved
by abolishing the aims and finding new ones to fit in with the
assumptions and habits.

It is very important to grasp the distinction between aims
or ideals, on the one hand, and forces which mould the
culture or soul, on the other.

Here is one illustration of that distinction, borrowed from
M. Denis Saurat, who develops it in his excellent booklet
Regeneration (Dent). He uses the analogy of two parts of the
inner life of man, which he calls the head and the masses.
The head is that part which is clear and precise, which knows
what it wants. The masses represent the impulses, feelings,
memories, dogmas and habits. The head has itself two parts:
the power which takes decisions, and a number of talents
which carry them out.

> "The relation between the head and the masses (the main
> distinction) is complicated. The head is only the concen-
> trated clarification of the masses. It can only act on them,
> because it represents them truly, because it is that part of
> themselves that they have clarified and of which they have

become fully conscious. But this is not always clear, and many a man in a crisis finds himself deciding and doing things of which he had never thought and which he would have believed himself incapable of doing. A new head has been thrown up by the masses in an emergency."

So writes Professor Saurat.

Power and freedom depend upon a certain harmony and mutual reinforcement between these two elements. They must also have their distinction. If all is masses there is no freedom; if all is head there is no power. Now, the same distinction and mutual aid or antagonism as we find in the single human being obtain also in a society. The aims and ideals of its members are no good alone; unless they are supported by the general habit of life and emotional patterns, the aims will always be defeated and there will be set up psychic and social conflict. This will grow until one is brought into line with the other. Professor MacMurray has repeated more than once that the influences which form a society are not so much its prevalent ideals but rather the way in which millions live and work, their feelings, attitudes, fears, hopes, loves and hates. Idealism usually makes a picture quite unrelated to these realities; certainly it is not the clarification of them.

We find the conflict we are talking about described in St. Paul's well-known account of his own problem and its solution, in the seventh and eighth chapters of the Epistle to the Romans. His aim, sincerely and strongly held, was to keep God's Law, but he found "another law in my members warring against the law of my mind" (his desire to obey the Law). The more he willed, the less he was able. The resolution of the conflict came with a transformation of his soul by the discovery of an outside power "the law of the Spirit of life in Christ Jesus."

If we use the term "soul" in its precise sense for this more hidden and formless part of our inner life, to distinguish it from that more conscious, deliberate part of our inner life, which is the spirit—and we do this when we talk about "saving our souls"—then we can see an analogy between the soul of the individual and the culture of a community. The aim or will of the individual is dependent for its power upon support in the bent of the soul; in society the effectiveness of policy depends upon its working in the same direction as the deepest cultural forces in it. It is not for nothing that spiritual writers have spoken of the culture of the soul and a famous book of devotion has the title *The Garden of the Soul.*

There are three main kinds of influences which mould the soul of a civilization, which is its culture. They are, first, its dogmas—the things it takes for granted about the nature of reality. These do not come into the field of discussion, but are presupposed in all discussions. Secondly, there are the things individuals and the mass of men do every day or regularly—the rituals. For example, it makes a difference whether a man begins the day with the newspaper or at his prayers or in the fields, or what is the regular kind of work one does or sees the majority of one's neighbours doing; whether periods of free time are marked by the closing of the banks, as on Bank holidays, or by the Holy Days of the Church. Thirdly, there is the structure and organization of society. This includes the order of rank, importance and status accorded to different kinds of persons, the occupations deemed more or less essential, central and normal; the values of different jobs and positions which affect men's views of what is a step up or a slip down the social scale.

Let us look at our culture, and see if we can detect a conflict between its aims and the forces which mould its soul. Of these forces, I shall have time to deal only with the first of the three main types—namely, the outlooks which have become so much a part of ourselves that we regard them as axiomatic. But, first of all, what are the aims of our Western, democratic, liberal culture—the thing we are struggling to defend in this War? I think they can in the main be reduced to four general ones.[1] The first is the pursuit of truth. This assumes that there is an objective truth about things to be discovered; that it can be reached and ought to be sought. We may learn all we should from Marx and Nietzsche and from the "sociologists of knowledge", who tell us that our approach to, and our apprehension of, truth are very much determined by our sociological situation and our interests therein. All this is very valuable, and has been too lightly obscured by our over-confident belief in the independent power of the reason; but it is a valuable corrective only because it seeks to identify and counteract the tendency to confuse our prejudices with our ideas of truth. European civilization has had as its intellectual ingredient the belief in man's power to eliminate bias and cultivate disinterestedness in finding out what is true. Science proceeded, in the days of its ascendancy, on the assumption that the personal factor which introduces an element of bias can be surmounted. This attitude, which we have taken far too much for granted as inevitable, is the opposite of the view that there is no objective truth but that all beliefs are a form of propaganda—something which is useful to a man or group struggling for power and position in the general flux. The habit of mind which believes that there is an objective truth to be striven for in face of temptations to make it an instrument of policy and advantage, is one of the marks of civilization. It is also this habit of mind which has underlain what was positive and fruitful in the desire for toleration, for freedom of opinion, of speech and of the Press; though it must be added that this freedom largely survives now with less genuine belief in truth and a more enfeebled idea of toleration than the convictions which inspired the beginning of the liberal era.

[1] In this section and in the following one, dealing with the assumption, upon which these aims were reared, I am summarizing an argument more fully developed in my *The Religious Prospect* (F. Muller, 1939).

A second characteristic of European culture is the conviction of a certain rightness for men and things and actions, which constitutes a ground of appeal from the self-interested desires of men and the conflicts of power they bring about. It assumes the notion of an absolute good and evil, even though codes of conduct are only relative and often misleading applications of that notion. Right and wrong have a metaphysical force, and are not merely serviceable conceptions in the struggle of life. This means that its existence itself is not sufficient justification for any event. The good is an attribute of a certain kind of life, and cannot be identified with the fact of life itself. Therefore might is no criterion of right. A successful agent is no judge in his own cause merely because his deed is a success. Mr. C. S. Lewis has shown that to eliminate ultimate standards from the judgment of human achievements leads to the disintegration of what is specifically human among created things. He calls it the Abolition of Man.[1] At the beginning of this century hardly anyone would have denied this fact of an objective norm of action, though already in the nineteenth century man like Nietzsche proclaimed that "a good War halloweth every cause", and Goethe expressed something very deep in the Teutonic mind which takes action as its own criterion, when he "corrected" the Johannine "*In the beginning was the Word*" and substituted "In the beginning was the deed". But to-day not only the philosophy of totalitarian politics, but some of the assumptions underlying education in the democracies, make ethics a view serviceable for action, instead of a criterion of action. The opposite conviction, which has been traditional for our culture, is that there is something worth dying—that is, giving up life—for. That something is the rightness which the thought of civilized life has called the good. This doctrine therefore contradicts the idea that superior force or mere success in perpetuating itself is the cultural criterion of any existence.

[1] *The Abolition of Man* (Rede Lecture).

We come thirdly to a legal extension of this second position, which is a mark of our culture. There is a Natural Law
in the constitution of existence which can be apprehended
by man, and to which appeal can be made against the positive
law of any particular State or legislature. The law is above the
State; the State is the embodiment and not the source of law.
The ruler is subject to a universal justice; he interprets and
administers it; but his will does not create it. This conception
of a law behind the ruling authority has had two interesting
embodiments. One was the Lord Chancellor, who represented the common, universal, standards of justice and acted
as check to local princes who were always tempted to regard
as ultimate the rules and actions they found convenient in
ruling their own local communities. The other expression
of this priority of the Law over the State is the separation of
the judiciary from the executive. Those who make and apply
the law from universal principles of right must not be
removable by the will of the executive power. The State, no
more than the individual or the group, may be judge in its
own cause. In this conception of law, which is the foundation
of equality before the law, we have a categorical denial of a
widespread attitude to-day that judicial decisions are those
that promote the policy of the prevalent governing power and
nothing else. This recognition of a law of human ordering
above all institutions is the expression in terms of law of a
much less abstract and more diffused conviction that persons
have a certain priority over institutions. Institutions exist for
persons, and not vice versa. There is in the last resort a
common right or reason, or Natural Law, to which the person
can appeal if his personal fulfilment is opposed by the demands of the institution. There have been many difficulties
in giving this principle a political application, but it remains
as the social expression of what is now called "the rights of
personality".

The fourth mark of our culture, so far as its aims are

concerned, has been the recognition of a universal character in all human beings. There is something common to all men as part of their essential nature, and this merits a proper moral respect—in spite of all differences of good and bad behaviour, of racial, national and class and sex variations. This essential element of man's being—"our common humanity", as it is called—is the basis of a certain meta-physical equality and underlies a respect for persons as such, in spheres both of personal relations and of social justice. It is something that man brings into his social relationships, but cannot be defined by them. Inequality is inherent in man as a natural and as a functioning part of the social order, in the family, in politics, in industry. Therefore, if man has no significance other than a social one, there can be no equality and no common element in the inner being of all men. Jacques Maritain has recently described this metaphysical and moral equality, which does not ignore the concrete and useful inequalities in men or make men equal only by con-sidering an abstract humanity divorced from real persons.[1] It demands equality in the fundamental rights of each to preserve the body, to found a family, to associate, privately to own material goods and to seek eternal life according to one's conscience, to have equality before the law; to partici-pate "free of charge" in the elementary goods needed for human life, so far as society can provide them. Recognition of this universal element in all men, which derives from a reality above and behind their actual place in social history, means that they occupy that place with an authority not dependent upon it. This is one of the foundations of demo-cracy, according to which no man may be treated only as subject to the authority of the body politic; all must have some part in framing the laws of that authority.

These are four marks of the more conscious aims of men in "the democracies". We know that such aims have been

[1] Essay on "Human Equality" in *Redeeming the Time* (Bles).

B

directly attacked by totalitarian philosophies and regimes. We do not see so clearly that they are in danger within "the democracies" themselves, not so much because the aims are weakly held, as because there are a number of influences in our culture which tell against them, and which we do not suspect of undermining them. Those aims became conscious as social principles in the modern period in the movements of emancipation from medieval and ancient outlooks. But they are developments of elements in those outlooks, and depend upon a great many assumptions, habits and social patterns which have been swept away in the modern humanist age. This is one of the tragedies of history. And we do not properly realize that the cultural transformations of the last two or three centuries have left the aims, which are the spirit of our Western civilization, without support in the soul of our culture. People have relied on the inherited culture underneath their aims, as if it were emerging to greater fullness from the restrictions of the past. This they called "Progress" or "Social Evolution". The men of the nineteenth century believed that the human race was on a historically guaranteed road, and that modern technical civilization was providing it with more efficient tools. Because they took their culture for granted—hardly thought about it—and did not refer the new powers to it, the vast forces of social change took charge, and human purposes were steadily moulded by the changes, instead of the other way round.[1] That is why the society of the twentieth century, as Christopher Dawson has pointed out, is not the kind of society the men of the nineteenth thought they were creating.[2] They were on the whole in the humanist, liberal tradition, and they believed they were merely giving man greater powers to embody that tradition. They looked upon their achievement as furthering the expansion of the individual personality. The decline of

[1] Cf. *A Time is Born*, by Garet Garrett and N. Beryaev, *The Meaning of History*, pp. 150 ff.
[2] *Enquiries in Religion and Culture*, p. 4.

that tradition is a tragedy; it is the withering of a flower torn from its soil.

What is the origin of this tradition, and what has happened to it in our time? The four aims which constitute its most conscious aspect did not originate with Christianity; they were aims or ideals in the classical Graeco-Roman world. But they came to be supported by a concrete culture only by reason of certain Christian presuppositions and patterns of behaviour. The first two of these aims, for instance—the belief in truth and in right and wrong—rest upon an outlook for which the central reality of the Universe transcends the temporal and historical process, and for which man has relations to this eternal reality as well as to his historic setting. Belief in truth and right withers as soon as men feel themselves to be only parts of an immanent flux. Man has no link with anything outside the process.

The notion of the person as having a certain priority over the temporal community—purposes which are not merely social purposes—was stamped upon men's minds not so much by positive teaching as by there being a counter-institution, the Church, whose very existence upheld the axiom that there are some spheres of life in which the writ of Caesar does not run. The whole European tradition of what we call and value as liberty derives from a culture in which no one power was supreme. And Rosenstock-Huessy has shown how deeply the dogma of the fundamental equality of men was impressed upon Europe by the rituals surrounding death and the commemoration of All Souls. The Christian conviction that men die equal was more potent than the humanist abstraction that men are born equal.

While it is not until the twentieth century that the pattern of European culture is radically threatened, there have been of course since the Renaissance several intellectual, political and religious revolts from the past of Europe. But they all assumed that the foundations of that culture were permanent.

The cult of the enlarged individual of the Enlightenment presupposed the pattern of community living of the Middle Ages. The philosophers of the seventeenth century, with their faith in man's glorious future through mathematical knowledge and clear ideas, just took for granted that their intellectual social stratum would continue to be fed and bred by a biological, domestic and craft basis of society that would look after itself and increase in strength. The Industrial Revolution was carried out by men whose cultural ideal was the country gentlemen. The early socialists were the champions of status for the artisans, which idea they inherited from the past, and the notion of corporate functional responsibility from the Guilds. Throughout this period, too, the family was believed in, even amid Capitalism, which did most to destroy it. All this means that just as the culture of a society is a slow growth, its decline is much slower than the rise and fall of movements which challenge its aims. The culture of European civilization is almost worn out; and other cultures of an entirely different order have taken its place.

We might say that all the things men strove for at the Renaissance were things Europe had learnt unconsciously from the eighth to the fifteenth century and from the Ancient World. And these were not impossible aims so long as the less deliberate parts of life, such as family, work, eating, social consciousness, regional and local health, status and exchange, had a certain natural vitality. They provided few intellectual problems, though there were plenty of practical ones. Man's activities arose naturally out of their needs.

When now we come to ask, What are the main forces that have moulded our modern culture and made it inimical to the aims that belong to European civilization? we must make a selection. I will mention three large-scale ones. First, in the matter of men's outlook on existence there has been a fundamental change. We may call it "the denial of the transcendent". The genuine religious outlook has always understood existence as constituted by an eternal world behind and related to the temporal world; it held that the process which marks everything in the created order is only to be given a meaning by reference to an abiding, transcendent source of being which, though not itself in process, is the origin of all things and their destinies. Religions differ in the way they regard this particular relation of eternity and time. For Christians it is embodied in the doctrine of the Creation, the Incarnation and Resurrection of Christ, and the Last Day, and in teaching about the Logos and about the Church as a new history transecting the old. But, on any view of this relation, man has his peculiar significance from the fact that he is in a unique relation to the eternal, while at the same time he is involved in the process of the earth's life and the sweep of human history.

Modern man, on the contrary, has come to know himself only as an item in the historic process, and to recognize no reality apart from that of the temporal world. This leads him to deal with life only in terms of relation to his environment, to the social whole, and to past and future. It makes him seek the key to the meaning of his existence in some layer of his own being—either his reason, his urges, his work, his society or his race. Denial of the transcendent obscures the really religious dogma that the person is, in Kierkegaard's phrase, "the point of intersection of time and eternity". From this complete change of outlook I derive the terrible paradox that modern man, who is in great control over things, is also carried along by a process he cannot control. A deep sense that social development has a momentum of its own, at variance with true human purposes, gives sensitive people the feeling that there is a doom on our civilization, quite apart from possibilities of unlimited destruction in war. We have lost the up-and-down dimension in existence—the penetration of eternity into time, the spiritual depth in all finite things—that can give meaning to the temporal process. And with this has disappeared not only the axiom that human life owes an obedience to the Divine Will, but also any conviction that there is a permanent structure of human life, relating man's material, mental and spiritual powers, an order which reflects the essential nature of man and must underlie all variations and adornments of his existence. There is therefore no test by which man can detect whether what is going on is in the truly human interest. And the more he is advised by the "human, all too human" sciences to adjust himself to his situation, the more he is like a minnow whirled along in an impersonal flood he has set flowing.

Then, in the second place, we have put all our confidence to control the drift of things in the rational and scientific method. But this provides only powerful instruments, it does not by itself give direction or determine purposes. There is a confused debate about this which should be cleared up. The scientific mind is one of the finest products of the human spirit. As Lewis Mumford puts it: "This displacement of limited egoistic wishes, this reference to common data and to objective methods of proof, open to all other competent men, is one of the real contributions of science to the human personality itself". And while our culture was relatively robust, the growing powers of the scientific mind were rightly hailed as possible aids in the betterment of human life. From the seventeenth to the nineteenth century men of science were learners from existence, and they worked from out of a culture whose ethical and human aims they believed in; they operated from a place on the earth which supported their life and that of all other men, in the non-rational, vital and personal parts of their existence. But then came the steady undermining of this culture on which they counted, and an exaggerated confidence that because the universe could be so well handled by reason and experiment, these would be able to control existence itself. But the total existence of man consists in all the activities of human beings in their concrete setting, and this includes so much that is not rationally to be apprehended. So it has come to be assumed that anything that could be done technically should be done technically, and that human life would be the better for it. One result is that we are mad for efficiency—for things that are useful for something else. What the whole equipment is for is some undated millennium in the future—an altar on which have been sacrificed perhaps more victims than on any other. Our vast technical civilization is providing more and more powerful means to do things and less opportunity for doing anything we can enjoy—that is to say, anything satisfying for its own sake. In particular it is supplying great sources of pure energy while the civilization it creates is eating up the sources of life in the earth, in local, regional and national growths. If you have its price in your pocket it will soon be easier to get a wireless set than a cabbage, a power-station than a house, or an aeroplane than a shirt.

Thirdly, the whole economic side of what is called "industrialism" has defeated the right and proper use of the machine. To condemn the machine is a romantic error and a theological mistake. But a civilization with machines that has to set up full employment as a social goal is one that has somehow divorced the activity by which men earn their living from the purposes for which they work. So we have to make more machine products in an expanding economy in a world where the spread of the industrial arts is making expansion for everybody arithmetically impossible. It also means that a man must turn more and more steel into machines to earn the price of a loaf of bread. Good food, good houses, good clothes—all these become too expensive in a world where the production of bigger technical and State equipment is given higher and higher priority. This is an ironic consequence of a development which, it was hoped, would give the masses of men what had before been the privilege of the sheltered classes.

These are three major factors which have formed the soul of modern man so that the aims he still professes are betrayed by a culture inimical to them. All three tendencies press him to regard events themselves as giving sanction to the ideas of right, of reason, of law, instead of having to be evaluated by them. A philosophy of expediency gradually instills itself into the mind. Thus is undone the whole civilized tradition of the Race.

All this points to the need of a renewal of our European culture which could use, instead of being debauched by, all the advantages of a century's technical achievement. It is a much bigger task than talking about bringing our existing civilization under more moral and political control. In fact this is impossible without the rebirth of the culture out of which the ethical and political aims of Western civilization have grown. In the lectures which follow other speakers will show what some elements in that culture are, what is happening to them to-day, and what such a rebirth as I have adumbrated calls for.

II. OUR CULTURE: ITS THOUGHT

by

H. A. Hodges

IT is natural that in these days of conflict and crisis there should be much talk of the breakdown with which European civilization seems to be threatened. Yet such talk, natural as it is, will do no good, and may do harm if it does not lead to a serious diagnosis of what is wrong. The aim of the present series of lectures is to help towards such a diagnosis by taking the various aspects of our trouble one by one; and it falls to me as a professed philosopher to trace the growing crisis as it appears in men's beliefs about the world and their place in it.

The civilization which is now tearing itself to pieces around us is that of a Europe in which, until very recently, the Christian Faith was almost everywhere publicly professed, and had been so for many centuries. For fifteen or sixteen centuries in the Mediterranean, and for a shorter but still lengthy period farther north, Christianity has been deeply entrenched in the seats of learning, in the favour of governments, in popular beliefs and customs. All our thoughts about human relationships, as well as the wider questions concerning human life and destiny, have been moulded by it. No one therefore need be surprised if the troubles by which Europe is now overtaken lead us to ask certain questions about Christianity. A world which believed and declared itself to be Christian is in danger of ruin: is there a relation, and if so what, between the ruin and the Christianity?

The question might be given a different twist by describing the facts more in detail. Christian influence was at its height in Europe not in recent times, but in the Middle Ages, when the Church, strong in its international hierarchy and its international language, its unbroken tradition and the prestige of the Roman name, possessed in addition an almost complete monopoly of education and of administrative and diplomatic skill. In every school and university, from the pulpit of every parish in Europe, there poured a constant stream of Christian propaganda, and there was nothing of nearly comparable power to set against it. Since the Renaissance things have changed. Learning and all the other cultural, social and political activities have become independent of the Church. They have developed fast and far in independence of her and often in opposition to her. Her voice in the modern world is only one among many voices, and sometimes sounds curiously archaic and somnambulistic. Broadly speaking, the growth of the modern world has kept pace with the decline of Christian influence. Is there a causal relation here? It is easy for the Christian to say that there is: that a world which was once stable and unified because it was Christian is now going to ruin because it is losing its Christianity. It is equally easy for someone else to say that the age of greatest Christian influence in Europe was the age of greatest ignorance and poverty, and that to-day the effect of surviving Christian ideas and organizations is at least as often destructive and reactionary as not.

How are we to decide this issue? There is only one way. We must examine more closely the extent to which, and the manner in which, Christianity has affected the minds of men in the various stages of European history.

1. *The Medieval Period.*

Medieval Europe was pre-eminently a Christian Europe, and there is a widespread tendency to regard its distinguishing characteristics, both good and evil, as products of Christian influence. Feudalism, the gild system, chivalry, scholasticism: all these have been claimed as resting in some peculiar way upon Christian principles. The first thing we must do is to recognize that this is a mistake. Christianity did not make the medieval world or its ideas. Medieval society sprang from causes inherent in an impoverished agricultural economy with primitive methods of production and distribution and harassed by military insecurity. These causes lie in a field remote from religion, and were at work before Christianity became a determinative force. Medieval learning is an inheritance from Greek and Roman sources, and neither in law nor in medicine nor in philosophy did Christianity originate anything radically new. What it did was to give the medieval world a peculiar critical consciousness of itself, a depth and height of consciousness, though it signally failed to give breadth. Let us take examples to show what this means.

Every social system is hierarchic in some degree: people differ in respect of the importance and creativeness of the work they do, the amount of authority or responsibility they carry. Medieval society was more hierarchic than most, and its hierarchy was more obviously functional than most. Threatened all along by poverty and danger, Europe had no time to spare for the upkeep of a merely decorative class or for the encouragement of activities which did not contribute substantially to the common good. Men did not carve out careers for themselves by free enterprise in a world of wide opportunity; they were born into a society organized for the fulfilment of certain specific functions in certain specific ways, and they lived and worked within this system in the place marked out for them by birth or assigned to them by training and initiation. Everyone had his place, and his rights and duties in his place. Everyone had a superior, up to the Pope and the Emperor, and no one was entirely at the mercy of his superior, since he could always hope for the protection of one power against another. It was a complex and yet a compact system, combining safety and freedom as well as they could be combined in the circumstances of the time.

What Christianity did was to teach men that this system of hierarchy and function, which was the framework of their lives, was merely one part of a more extensive system of hierarchy and function which embraced all reality, and thus to give it a sanction and a meaning through its relation to a principle wider than itself. All reality centred on God, supremely real, supremely wise, supremely good, lacking nothing, dependent on nothing, incommensurable with all but himself, so that even the wonder and richness of the world he has created cannot add anything to his majesty and blessedness. Yet from God's free, unconstrained, unmerited love this world has sprung, and to him it owes both that it is and what it is, and no smallest detail of it can exist for a moment without him. Though the gulf between creature and Creator is infinite, yet the glory of God's being is reflected in his works according to their kind (what else could their being be but a reflection of his from whom it comes?), and more so in some than in others, from formless matter which is hardly distinguishable from nothing, through fully formed material things to things possessed of life and motion, to man, to the bodiless intelligences, numberless and inconceivably diverse, which see God and see the world in God and live only to see and worship and serve. Man stands midmost in the great array, lowliest of spirits and alone dependent on an animal body, noblest of animals and alone capable of the knowledge of God, weak and ignorant yet aspiring to highest power and knowledge, made for an end outside and above himself, and incapable of being even himself unless he attains it.

In this graded world everything has its place and is good in its place, and the divine order which assigns to man his position of mingled humility and glory is carried out into the details of human life and society. Thus parenthood, lordship and all forms of rank and authority spring from the throne of

God. Not only the natural order, but the supernatural order and the gospel of redemption fall within this scheme. What does the Fall mean but that man, in trying to rise above his place, fell below it, and lives now with passions disordered and intellect darkened, a stranger and afraid in the world he was to have ruled under God? But he has been redeemed and raised to a higher glory than he had before through the coming of God in human nature: and the economy of redemption flows through a society, the Church, not of natural origin but founded and guided from above, itself a rich complex of ranks and functions like the natural society amid which it lives, yet throughout of a higher dignity in so far as the eternal end which it serves transcends the temporal end to which civil and cultural institutions look.

In a society thus conscious of man's twofold dignity it is not surprising that all learning was ordered to man's twofold end, to the relief of his estate on earth and to the worship of God. In a medieval university the degrees were all in subjects relating directly to man or to God. "Science" as we know it now, inquiry into the laws of the physical world for the sake of knowledge or of power, was not found there; such physical science as did exist, chiefly astronomy, was partly utilitarian (fixing the calendar and aiding navigation) and partly metaphysical (the harmony of the heavens declares the glory of God), and was not a complete degree course in itself. One studied Arts, and then Law, or Medicine, or Theology. Philosophy itself was a meditation on God, a rational explication of theology, a clarification of faith.

It is a mistake to think of St. Thomas Aquinas as a typical medieval philosopher. He was an innovator, and Gilson has even called him the first of the moderns. What is new in him is precisely his emphasis, tempered and relative though it is, on the world as the commensurate object of man's intellect, and on man's power and duty to study and master it. A more typical medieval thinker is St. Anselm, and in his *Proslogion* the spirit of medieval philosophy is vividly to be seen. Not merely the argument, but even the literary form of the work is significant: it is a treatise on metaphysics in the form of an address by the inquiring soul to God. He sets himself to meditate, to turn from himself and his petty concerns to the contemplation of God. As his meditation progresses he sees that it was for the vision of God that he was created, and also that he has never had that vision, never fulfilled the end of his being. He sees that this failure is due to sin, and can never be set right but by an act of redemption. God himself must recreate in Anselm the lost capacity to know God, that faith may grow into understanding; and he prays God to do this. But then he sees that he could not even have made this prayer if he did not at least believe that God is, and that he is supremely desirable, a Being than whom no greater can be conceived. Then follow two paragraphs of close argumentation to show that the very fact that we can think of God in this way proves his-existence, so that the knowledge of him is actually implicit in our faith, waiting only to be enucleated. Then at the end the argument slides back into praise. "So thou, O Lord my God, dost exist in so true a sense that thou canst not even be thought not to exist; and this is as is fitting." Metaphysics as an incident in the course of a religious meditation; philosophy springing from worship and returning to it, with no sense of any barrier or boundary between the two—that is the spirit of medieval thinking.

2. *The Renaissance Period and Age of Reason.*

The same economic and social processes which brought the medieval order into existence brought also its slow dissolution. A system bred of poverty and insecurity gave way before the growth of wealth in the towns, and the increasing power of centralized governments imposing peace, law and security over wide territories. Merchant enterprise, sometimes alone and sometimes actively assisted by governments,

reached out beyond Europe and inaugurated the age of overseas exploration and colonization. This reacted upon Europe,
where wealth and power increased more rapidly than ever.
The conditions were thus created for a great outburst of
cultural energy, which showed itself first in the arts and then
in the momentous discovery of the scientific method and the
inauguration of the intellectual revolution of modern times.
It is natural that the thought of such an age should move on
different lines from that of the Middle Ages, and that the
form assumed and the part played by Christianity should
also be different.

The prevailing impression on men's minds throughout this
period is that of the immensity and variety of the universe,
and the wealth of natural resources awaiting development on
this planet. In the matter of geographical exploration and
overseas expansion it was generally felt that it was a wide
world with room in it for all. The attempts of one or two
States to stake out exclusive claims in certain areas were
ignored and frustrated by their strong rivals. It was to be a
free field for all and no favours, and those who failed in one
enterprise could always contrive another. As time went on and
reflection on matters of trade gave rise to the infant science of
political economy, it was taken for granted that this free
expansion could go on indefinitely to the advantage of all.
The eventual closing of the frontier and the complete appro-
priation one day of all the world's resources were not foreseen, and therefore the coming struggle for markets was not
foreseen either. In a world with room for all, each can grow
rich without impoverishing others. There is a natural harmony of interests which the philosophers and economists of
the period admiringly contemplate.

In the world of thought and imagination a like unlimited
range of opportunity seemed open, and this gives the tone to
the cultural history of the period. It is an age of free experiment, when everyone lets his own genius lead him where it

can, and each new decade sees new possibilities explored.
Tradition is at a discount. The unity of all knowledge in its
common concern with man and God is no more thought of.
Art and literature, philosophy, science, each pursue their
way in what seems at first to be independence. Only a later
age will find that it is really chaos. For the present the result
is an immense expansion of knowledge, both of man and of
the world around him. It is the age of Shakespeare, whose
mind reflected the whole world of human character and
destiny, and, having exhausted the worlds of ancient and
medieval Europe, imagined new ones in unknown countries
and islands. The one thing in human experience which
Shakespeare does not understand and cannot convincingly
depict is religion (his priests are nice old men who quote
Seneca); that is, the one thing missing from his view of life is
the one thing which gave unity to everything in such a poet
as Dante. A like voracious curiosity and a like weakening of
the religious strain characterize the work of the scientists and
their interpreters, such as Bacon and Locke.

By the end of the seventeenth century these tendencies
were crystallizing into a widely accepted set of doctrines.
Man, it was held, is the destined master of nature, and his
mastery will be established through the advance of knowledge.
Knowledge is the way to power, freedom, breadth and depth
of understanding—all that makes life worth while. Knowledge cannot grow without freedom of research and freedom
of speculation, and this must be provided for and encouraged.
Hence we must make a principle of toleration. Free re-
searches in different fields will often lead in divergent directions, and while that is all right for the researchers themselves,
the world in general will need a comprehensive survey or
synthesis. Philosophy is to be called upon to provide this—
a herculean task which only exceptional philosophers of the
calibre of Leibniz or Kant could discharge with any honour.

Where is God in all this? What was Christianity doing in

these centuries? Men did not cease to believe in God or even
to worship him, but they did both in rather a new way. As in
the Middle Age, Christianity was able to interpret and enrich
the prevailing ideas by giving them a place in a wider scheme;
but this time the synthesis was made on lines which meant
leaving out or overlooking important elements in Christianity
itself.

The basis of the new scheme was the immensity, and at the
same time the harmony, of the world order; not a hierarchic
order now, but an order of natural law, and also an order of
purposeful contrivance and adaptation, wherein everything
was so constituted that by following its own impulse it
furthered the harmony and beauty of the whole. In this
order men saw the union of infinite power with infinite
wisdom and goodness, and during all our period the progress
of science seemed more and more to enforce this conclusion.
Astronomy in particular was called in evidence, and the
astronomers themselves were forward in giving testimony.
Thus Newton, who laid the foundations of all modern physics
and astronomy, believed that space was God's *sensorium*,
and ended his *Principia* with a chapter proving the necessity
of God as First Mover to devise and set going the mechanism
of the solar system. (The nebular theory which was to enable
Laplace to dispense with "that hypothesis" had not yet been
born.) Thus encouraged, Addison could versify the nineteenth Psalm, carefully unrolling before us the details of the
planetary and sidereal heavens, and ending in an ecstasy of
rational conviction:

> In Reason's ear they all rejoice,
> And utter forth a glorious voice,
> For ever singing, as they shine,
> "The hand that made us is divine".

With him a host of eighteenth-century hymn-writers let
themselves go in praise of the God who

> . . . fixed this floating ball,

C

who set the heavens in order, who

> . . . formed the stars, those heavenly flames,
> He counts their numbers, calls their names;
> His wisdom's vast, and knows no bound,
> A deep where all our thoughts are drowned.

They saw his power and his wisdom together in the majesty of natural law:

> Praise the Lord, for he hath spoken;
> Words his mighty voice obeyed;
> Laws, which never shall be broken,
> For their guidance hath he made.

But they saw these divine attributes also in the processes of life and growth. Astronomy was linked with natural history, for this is the great age of the argument from design; and this too is transmuted into praise in the gloriously confident nature-hymns of the eighteenth century.

> He makes the grass the hills adorn,
> And clothes the smiling fields with corn;
> The beasts with food his hands supply,
> And the young ravens when they cry.

Christianity seized also upon the second great principle of our period, the principle of free thought and toleration, and set it in a new light. To say that Christian influence first established this principle would be to say too much; it was part of the rationalistic philosophy which arose out of the hopes and ambitions of the time. Once established, however, Christianity could exhibit it as a kind of reverence for reason, which is the image of God in every man. "The spirit of man is the candle of the Lord", and not only the spirit of orthodox Christians. Toleration began to appear as an act of humility (willingness to listen and learn) and charity (unwillingness to prejudge). A good expression of this attitude may be found in Chapters 26 and 27 of *Robinson Crusoe*, especially Crusoe's conversation with the French priest at the opening of Chapter 27, which ends with the aphorism that "there is no heresy in abounding with charity".

In this optimistic atmosphere the more challenging parts of Christian teaching tended to be lost. The Fall and its consequences were frequently forgotten or denied, and a different version of the past was put forward, which exhibited man's history as a process of natural healthy growth and maturation in a harmonious world where everything is for the best. Man is not fallen, but risen and rising. He does not need redemption, he can make his way forward by himself, provided only that he has knowledge. If God can do anything for him, it must be to reveal certain fundamental truths; but even so this revelation may turn out to be little more than a republication of truths which were known to the wise men of old, to Hermes Trismegistus or Zoroaster or the Druids, and are known to-day by the light of nature to all men of sense. This line of thought first appears with Ficino in the fifteenth century, passes into the natural religion school and deism, and ends in Herder, who reinterprets the word "revelation" to make it mean "intuitive insight", thus making it man's own achievement. The Christian sacred story can then be rewritten as the tale of the progress of religious genius among the Jews. The circle is closed. The very idea of a divine action upon man (as distinct from man's own actions considered as divine) begins to be resented as an "interference" with the majestic process of moral growth, an infringement of man's free dignity and a breach of natural law. God now stands over against man, and man looks him squarely in the face and forbids him to trespass. Kant can say that to rise above the fear of natural forces and catastrophes is in a manner to rise above God—above God as manifested in nature—and the high point is reached in the naïve unintentional blasphemy of the *Hymne à l'Être Suprême* by Desorgues.

> Tout émane de toi, grande et première cause,
> Tout s'épure aux rayons de ta divinité;
> Sur ton culte immortel la morale repose,
>   Et sur les moeurs la liberté.

Pour venger leur outrage et ta gloire offensée,
L'auguste Liberté, ce fléau des pervers,
Sortit au même instant de ta vaste pensée
    Avec le plan de l'univers.

Dissipe nos erreurs, rends-nous bons, rends-nous justes,
Règne, règne au delà du tout illimité;
Enchaîne la nature à tes decrets augustes,
    Laisse à l'homme la Liberté.

"We will allow you to give us knowledge, but not to control our will. Keep off the grass." A God whom we address in this way is fast becoming a mere lay figure. In the same year in which Desorgues published his hymn, Fichte was publishing his *Wissenschaftslehre* and reducing God to the consensus of rational human wills. The philosophy of immanence has arrived.

Of course this development was not allowed to pass without challenge. The challenge was the Reformation. Against the humanism of Ficino or Erasmus arises the uncompromising fideism of Luther and the Calvinist proclamation of the sovereignty of God. The march of humanism and science goes on, hardly delayed for a moment, but all through the seventeenth and eighteenth centuries we see a series of rearguard actions by Protestantism, of which Methodism in Britain is a notable example, and the series goes on through the nineteenth century to the present day. The protests have all been ineffective in the long run, for two obvious reasons. First, they had no positive alternative to what they attacked. Humanism was reading the signs of the times and addressing itself to the present task; the Christian protest hardly amounted to more than an attempt to shoot the pianist. Second, there were humanists in the Protestant ranks themselves. Beside Luther stood Melanchthon, and the movement in general often appealed to "sound learning" in its polemic against Catholicism. If you appeal to reason in support of an irrationalist doctrine, the argument will refuse the conclusion. Protestant controversy trained men in the use of weapons of scholarship which were then trained upon Protestantism itself with deadly effect.

3. *The Modern Crisis.*

Already in the Age of Reason we can see the beginnings of developments which have grown into the first-class cultural crisis of to-day. For our present purpose it will be convenient to single out three aspects of the crisis for examination.

(*a*) Among the most representative present-day thinkers the hierarchic order of being has pretty well been lost to view, and God himself has either vanished with it or become a pretentious name for the universe and man. Our attitude to life is this-worldly and our philosophies are immanentist. One result of this is that man's deepest concern has been re-oriented as it were at right angles to its previous direction. Picture man standing on earth, with the variety of nature all around him and God above him. His attention will be divided between the horizontal and the vertical views. Medieval man stood in this position, and was sure that it was the vertical view which chiefly mattered. Man to-day is hardly aware of the vertical line at all, his outlook is horizontal. But that means that his imagination has been possessed by a new problem and a new drama: not now the drama of God and man, but that of man and nature. What is man's place in nature? Are they akin? Is nature the product of a shaping power which is somehow related to man's own reason? Is it a meaningless assembly of brute facts in which man is an insignificant accident? These questions haunt not only the philosophy but also the literature of the nineteenth century. They replace in large measure the religious concern which bulked large in previous periods. They are the theme on which the hopes and ambitions of men are based, and sometimes also their despairs.

O Dieu, parais, éclaire un si sombre univers. . . .
—Hélas, que l'homme en pleurs tende ses bras ouverts,
Ou qu'il crispe son poing frénétique, et blasphème,
La matière se meut en sa stupidité,
L'affreuse solitude est à jamais la même,
Et l'homme seul répond à l'homme épouvanté.[1]

(b) With a free field for hypothesis and experiment, and latterly with rich public endowments, science has gone ahead magnificently in its own proper enterprise of detecting the laws of nature. But it has had by-products of questionable value. The habit of scientific thinking itself has set a premium on the abstract calculating intelligence, and led to a partial atrophy of that side of the mind by which human situations are understood and human values recognized. Further, scientific knowledge has been translated into machinery and has made possible the industrial system of to-day, with its demonstrated capacity to manipulate natural forces for human ends and its besetting temptation to manipulate human beings for economic ends. Even in the eighteenth century the idea of *l'homme machine* had been canvassed as a striking speculation. The nineteenth-century mechanists undertook to prove it true, and industrialism and the social and political systems thrown up by industrialism are threatening to make it true.

(c) Philosophy, as might have been expected, has failed in the superhuman task of synthesis which was set it. It has lost courage, and cannot guide other studies because it lacks unity and direction itself. The principle of unlimited exploration and experimentation in all directions has not led to chaos in science, because the course of research has been controlled by empirical facts. False theories are tested, refuted and dropped. In philosophy the effect was different. The hold of tradition was loosened, and a crop of theories of new types, and diverse from one another, gained currency. Each was at best partial, yet because of the expectation that philosophy

---

[1] *Désespoir en Dieu*, by Paul Bourget.

was a synthesizing agent these partial theories were often stretched to cover or seem to cover wide fields of knowledge. The age of system-building set in, the age of encyclopaedias; and all kinds of philosophers offended, a positivist like Comte as well as an idealist like Hegel. Critique and iconoclasm had free play as well as constructive speculation, and often with better justification, for there was indeed much in the tradition of philosophy which had been too easily taken for granted and called for reassessment. The total result was a greater variety of opinions among philosophers than had ever been seen since Hellenistic times, and in the end the different schools and traditions have largely ceased even to understand one another.

The next stage was inevitable. Philosophy in the last hundred years has been full of tendencies towards subjectivism, relativism, pragmatism—tendencies which cast doubt upon the possibility of objective truth for man. Sometimes it is only philosophy itself which comes under suspicion; the positive sciences are left standing, though without the extra width and depth which philosophy has been supposed to give. But philosophy itself has been able to strike damaging blows at the credit of science and history, and in its own fall it may drag them down too. Then the result is a general scepticism and indifferentism. Nor can the process end here. Such scepticism undermines faith in thought and strips man of his mythologies and convictions; but it does not remove or weaken the passions which these mythologies and convictions once served to canalize and discipline. The plunging steeds of Plato's simile find their charioteer weakening, shaken by secret doubt and indecision. At last he throws the reins upon their necks and gives them their head. That is what is meant by thinking with one's blood, the maxim of the movement which has ruled Europe in arms for five years. Nazism is not the fancy of a small coterie, it is a mass movement, and the armed conquest of the Reich may prove to be not the end of the fight against Nazi doctrine, but the beginning. Nor is it evident that this is the only form which the cultural degeneration has taken or will take.

Of course this movement of degeneration is not the whole history of our culture in the last 150 years. If it had been, there would be nothing left by now. Europe is kept in being by survivals from earlier ways of life and thought, carried on the lasting foundation of natural human relationships and healthy common sense which no amount of corruption on the higher levels can destroy. Medieval ideas survive or are remembered by groups and individuals. The optimistic humanism of the Age of Reason sets the fashion of thought and feeling for multitudes who have not seen its weakness and have never been caught into the rhythm of scepticism and despair. Hence it is still possible to make play even now with ideas of natural law in the medieval sense, with hopes of progress and declarations of the rights of man. The slogans of freedom and opportunity are still potent. Science itself in its own sphere is a healthy activity, and its influence is often health-giving—upholding standards of intellectual rigour, honesty, thoroughness and devotion to the task in hand, which might with advantage be more widely diffused than they are. But we may well wonder whether these ideals, which still prevail in our conscious thinking, are not in fact being undermined by the process of dissolution which is the peculiar feature of these days, and whether we may not be like the men of late antiquity who went down under the barbarian darkness still professing their belief in deathless Rome.

Christianity, too, is still a factor in life and thought, though in a somewhat curious way. The adjustment reached by Christianity with the medieval world, the Reformation protest and the humanistic Christianity of a later age, are all preserved in the ecclesiastical institutions and traditions which they have moulded. Indeed, the first two have undergone a certain revival as the inherent weakness of modern humanism has become more apparent. But what have any of these forms of Christianity to say to an age of crisis like ours ? Either they adhere to the fundamental principles of modern humanism, which make God unnecessary though without always noticing it; or they stand boldly for the reality and sovereignty of God, but in ways which are relevant to a past situation and state of man. If we try to conceive what else they might do, it is not easy. What is there for Christianity to say, except either to comfort the suffering and disillusioned world with the assurance that its hopes and ideals are divinely underwritten and will yet prevail, or else to interpret the present catastrophes as God's judgment through history on humanistic presumption? It is true that there is one further thing which it theoretically might do. It might say to this shaken world, as the Holy Ghost said to Israel of old, that God's judgment is judgment in mercy, and that beyond destruction there is restoration. It might even give some hint of the nature of the new life that lies beyond the present shadow of death. But in practice how could Christianity do this without having itself lived through the death and seen the beginning of the things to come? To speak a positive word to our condition, the Church would need to have seen into the future.

Let us remember again that Christianity did not create medieval society, but found it and was able to accept and bless it. Christianity did not create the age of humanism, but saw it taking shape and was able to help it into existence and enrich its mind and life, though ultimately at a cost to Christianity itself. The inherent dialectic of humanism has now taken a turn which has led to the increasing frustration of humanistic hopes and the increasing alienation of culture from Christianity as well as from its own best traditions. It is natural to draw from this brief survey of the past two conclusions with regard to the future, and with these I will end.

(*a*) Chaos and dissolution will not last for ever, and sooner or later a new stable society will take shape. There is no reason to think that this, any more than its predecessors, will or could be created by Christian initiative. It will result from the operation of social forces in accordance with the laws, still imperfectly known, which govern such processes. It will stand over against Christianity as a given objective fact.

(*b*) There is no decisive reason as yet to think that the new order, when it comes, will be one which Christianity cannot accept and bless, as it did earlier orders, by setting its governing principles in a wider context and relating them to the structure of all existence, which flows from God. But if this happens, it will not be any form of Christianity now known that will perform the work. Connected with existing forms it may be, perhaps by lineal descent, but it will have been shaped by the same forces which will have shaped society at large, and only so can it be fit to speak to that society.

Such reflections as these may serve to moderate both the confidence of those Christians who think it is for them and their existing Churches to put the world right, and the macabre gusto of the neo-Christian prophets of doom. We may rather be led to see that both society and the Church are in God's hands, that both alike are under judgment, and that for both alike mercy may yet rejoice against judgment.

III. THE CRISIS OF CHRISTIAN CULTURE: EDUCATION

by

CHRISTOPHER DAWSON

I DO not think there is any need for me to insist on the fundamental thesis that the present crisis of Western civilization is due to the separation of our culture from its religious basis. I have been saying little else for the last fifteen years. But I think people are still not sufficiently aware of how great the responsibility of education has been in this disastrous process, and that the educationalists themselves have not really faced the disconcerting fact that the more education has advanced, at least quantitatively, the more our civilization has become secularized, so that the separation of our culture from its religious basis seems to be directly related to the spread of universal education.

Nor was this due to people being unaware of the danger. It was recognized from the beginning not merely by exceptionally religious people but by politicians and men of affairs. The Duke of Wellington, with his usual horse sense, put the whole thing in a nutshell when he said, "Take care what we are about, for unless you base all this on religion you are only making so many clever devils".

But the Duke of Wellington was not an educationalist, and his opinions were dismissed by the representatives of progressive ideas as the views of a reactionary, which indeed they were. Nevertheless he was justified, and we see to-day what a mess these clever devils have made of our world. No doubt the real source of the evil is to be found not in the universalization of education, but in the destruction of the old hierarchy of Divinity, Humanity and Natural Science that

was the tradition of European higher education. The real
evil of popular education was not so much its secularism, but
its Utilitarian character, which led to the progressive discard-
ing of all non-secular elements and motives. It is true that in
this country and in America we had a sort of alliance between dogmatic religion and secular utilitarianism which was
characteristic of the Victorian and nineteenth-century com-
promise. But it was an unnatural alliance which was incapable of withstanding the growing pressure of secularist culture. At the same time that this bleak Utilitarianism was
being replaced by a more humanist ideal of popular education, humanism itself was losing its prestige and its influence
on higher education. As the idea of culture becomes divorced
alike from religion and life, its social significance rapidly disappeared, until to-day we are witnessing a regular war against
culture and the apotheosis of the Common Man and the
Little Man and the Tough Guy—a regular pantheon of strange
gods who are emerging from some underworld of culture in
the half-light between the old European day and the dark
night of total barbarism. I do not think our civilization will
be saved from this fate by the quantitative progress of education on the existing lines: that is to say, by more education
given to more people for longer and longer periods. Indeed,
the extension of public education—that is to say, the attempt
of a single uniform educational system to mould the whole
mind of the whole community by a single all-embracing
educational system—only increases the mass-mindedness of
modern society without raising its cultural standards or
deepening its spiritual life.

It is possible that after the war we shall see a great intensi-
fication of educational effort, especially in the East and in the
non-European world. But behind this there will be a strong
competitive socio-political motive similar to that which inspired the educational efforts of the Soviets during the past
twenty years. At its best this means the raising of the standard

of life for all the backward and exploited peoples and classes; at its worst it may mean no more than the mass conditioning of populations for purposes of power politics. But in either case there is the same danger of an over-emphasis on the utilitarian motive and a neglect of the deeper spiritual forces which have been the creative element in all the great cultures of the past, whether Christian or non-Christian.

In the West, however, we have always passed through this phase. The economic man has become a commonplace to our great-grandfathers, and the utilitarians are more remote than the pre-Raphaelites. The time has come for us to retrace our steps, to see what we have lost in two centuries of economic progress and world conquest, and to consider how we can recover contact with the essential realities on which the existence of our civilization depends. If we admit, as I think we all do in principle, that Western culture was a Christian creation, that Europe is the daughter of Christendom, we ought to pay much more attention to this truth in our educational theory and practice than we have done in the past. I don't think we can say that the average young man or woman leaves their school or university with any clear conception of this fact. Taken in its widest sense, education is simply the process by which the new members of a community are initiated into its ways of life and thought from the simplest elements of behaviour or manners up to the highest tradition of spiritual wisdom. Christian education is therefore an initiation into the Christian way of life and thought, and for 1,200 years, more or less, the peoples of Europe have been submitted to this influence. The process has been intensive at some points, superficial at others, but taking it as a whole it may be said that nowhere else in the history of mankind can we see such a mighty stream of intellectual and moral effort directed through so many channels to a single end. However incomplete its success may have been, there is no doubt that it has changed the world, and no one has any right

to talk of the history of Western civilization unless he has
done his best to understand its doing and its methods.

But on the whole it has not been done. It has been neglected both by the historians and by the educationalists who
have tended to approach their subjects from a different point
of view. It is true that a treatment of history which is openly
hostile or contemptuous of Christian culture, like that of
Gibbon, is usually regarded as biased, but it is quite possible
to write of European culture as of national history leaving the
Christian tradition entirely out of the picture without the
average reader realizing that anything is missing. Nevertheless it was that tradition that conditioned the whole development of culture from the fifth to the nineteenth century, and
which created the standards of value and the vision of reality
which inspired its most characteristic achievements. To-day
religious education is apt to be considered a kind of extra
insecurely tacked on to the general educational structure, not
unlike a Gothic church in a modern housing estate. But in
the past it was the foundation on which the whole edifice of
culture was based, and which was deeply embedded below the
surface of social consciousness.

For from the beginning Christian education was conceived
not so much as learning a lesson, but as initiation into a new
life or, still more, as an initiation into a mystery. The early
manuals of Christian education, like the *Cathetical Discourses*
of St. Cyril or the *De Cathechizandis Rudibus* of St. Augus-
tine, all stress the esoteric character of the teaching. For
example, at the beginning of St. Cyril of Jerusalem's *Discourses* we read the following notice: "These Cathetical
lectures thou mayest put into the hands of the candidates for
Baptism and of baptised believers, but by no means of
Catechumens nor of any others who are not Christians as
thou shalt answer to the Lord. And if thou takest a copy of
them write this in the beginning, as in the sight of the
Lord". Christian education was something that could not be

conveyed by words alone, but which involved a discipline of
the whole man; a process of catharis and illumination
which centred in the sacred mysteries, and which was embodied in a cycle of symbolism and liturgical action.

Thus Christian education was not only an initiation into
the Christian community, it was also an initiation into another
world: the unveiling of spiritual realities of which the natural
man was unaware and which changed the meaning of existence. And I think it is here that our modern education—
including our religious education—has proved defective.
There is in it no sense of *revelation*. It is accepted as instruction—sometimes as useful knowledge, often as tiresome
task work in preparation for some examination, but nowhere
do we find that joyful sense of the discovery of a new and
wonderful reality which inspired true Christian culture. All
true religious education leads up to the contemplation of
Divine Mysteries, and where this is lacking the whole
culture becomes weakened and divided. It may be objected
that this is the sphere of worship and not of education; but it
is impossible to separate the two, since it was largely in the
sphere of worship that the Christian tradition of education and
culture arose and developed. The first Christian education
was the initiation into the Divine Mysteries in the liturgical
sense, and it brought with it a development of religious poetry
and music and art which was the first-fruits of Christian
culture. It is perhaps difficult for us to appreciate the educational significance of this, because the Christian liturgy and
its associated literature and art are still accepted as a living
element in our contemporary religious life, so that we do not
at once realize how different is the position it holds in our
culture from that which it held in the past.

At the present day the Church is but one institution among
a whole series of cultural organs which compete with one
another to form public opinion—the cinema and the wireless,
drama and fiction, the Press and the advertisement industry,

not to mention the youth movements and the political parties. But in the past, for whole centuries, and especially for the common people, the Church covered the whole orbit of culture, and it was only in the Church that the ordinary man found instruction, inspiration and spiritual sustenance. The churches still stand as the most striking objects in the European landscape, whether they dominate the cities, like Chartres and Lincoln, or whether they are lost in the countryside, like the village churches of England. But in either case they are the vital centres of the communities to which they belong. We must see them as they were in the days of their glory—glowing with colour, rich with sculpture, and filled with the music and dramatic action of the liturgy—powerhouses of the spirit—to realize the place they once held in the life of a people which was in other respects far poorer than it is to-day. Yet even to-day the churches in their comparatively derelict condition are by no means negligible in their influence on culture. To quote my own experience, I should say that I learnt more—much more—during my school days from my visits to the cathedral at Winchester than I did from the hours of religious instruction in school. That great church, with its tombs of the Saxon kings and the medieval statesmen-bishops, gave one a much greater sense of the magnitude of the religious element in our culture and the depths of its roots in our national life than anything one could learn from books. Nor was it merely a question of widening one's historical sense; it also deepened one's spiritual sense of religion as an objective reality far transcending one's private experience. And if this can be so even to-day, how much more in the past, when the cult of the saints and the holy places consecrated the whole historical and geographical context of culture and gave every social relation and activity its appropriate religious symbolism.

In northern Europe this accumulated treasure of religious symbolism was dispersed by the Reformation, which destroyed the liturgical character of popular culture and at the same time caused a great breach in the historical continuity of Christian tradition. Nevertheless the Reformation did not by any means undervalue the importance of religious education. On the contrary, the Reformers regarded their work largely as a reform or restoration of Christian education, which corresponded on the religious side to the renaissance of classical learning on the part of the humanists. Back to the Bible, the Bible only and the Bible for all: these were the slogans of the new religious education which so profoundly transformed our culture in the sixteenth and seventeenth centuries. And this involved important changes of psychological approach. It emphasized the literary element in education at the expense of the aesthetic, and it increased the importance of the individual as against the community. Wherever the Protestant tradition of education had free play —in Scotland, Puritan England, Geneva and New England, for example, it had a marked effect in increasing the literacy of the common people and in developing individualism, moral activism, and independence of judgment, though this was paid for by losses in other directions which showed themselves in the growing impoverishment of the communal life of society.

Volumes might be written on the social consequences of this divergence between the two traditions of Christian education—the liturgical Catholic and the Biblical Protestant. But they have not been written, so far as I am aware, and even in the discussions that have arisen on the possibility of an agreed syllabus of religious education this aspect of the question has been little regarded. The divergence was no doubt to some extent reduced by the strong influence of humanist education on Catholic and Protestant alike. Moreover, the two traditions influenced one another even at the period when religious disagreement was sharpest. Thus the Catechism, which from the sixteenth century almost to the

D

present day was the regular method of religious instruction, was of Protestant origin, but has become no less characteristic of modern Catholic religious education, while from the other side the Jesuit system of education exercised a considerable influence on Protestant grammar schools and academies.

But if the combined influence of Renaissance and Reformation made for the wider diffusion of literary culture and the intellectualizing of religious education, it also tended to increase the practical and utilitarian elements of culture. Both the Byzantine East and the medieval West had shared the same ideal of contemplation and spiritual vision as the supreme end and justification of all human culture: an ideal which finds classical expression in St. Thomas and Dante. But from the fifteenth century onwards culture and education became increasingly concerned with the claims of active life. The humanist ideal of an all-round cultivation of man's physical and intellectual abilities was brought into relation with the Protestant ideal of what Troeltsch has called secular or *innerweltlicher* ascetism—of sanctification by the diligent exercise of man's "calling"—of doing his duty in the state of life in which it has pleased God to call him. And this in turn led to the cultivation of the economic virtues of thrift and industry and to the acquisition of "useful knowledge " as the main end of education. There can be no doubt that secular Utilitarianism was the direct product and heir of the religious Utilitarianism that developed on the soil of Protestant, and specifically of Puritan, culture; for though Bentham himself was a disciple of the French Enlightenment, he was but the rationalizer of the movement, and its most characteristic types are a real native product of Protestant culture. Now, while this tradition, which we may call the tradition of Samuel Smiles, generated a great force of moral and practical energy, it was also responsible for the harsh and unattractive character of modern culture. One of the greatest Victorian educationalists—Matthew Arnold—was never tired of insisting on this, and, unlike most of his modern successors, he was not afraid to trace it back to its theological roots. "The period which is now ending for England," he wrote, "is that which began when, after the sensuous tumult of the Renaissance, Catholicism being discredited and gone, our serious nature desired as had been foretold 'to see one of the days of the Son of Man' and did not see it but men said to them see here and see there, and they went after the blind guides and followed the false direction, and the actual civilization of England and America is the result. A civilization with many virtues, but without lucidity of mind and without largeness of temper. And now we English, at any rate, have to acquire them, and to learn the necessity for us, 'to live', (as Emerson says) 'from a greater depth of being'. The sages and the saints alike have always preached this necessity; the so-called practical people and men of the world have always derided it. In the present collapse of this wisdom we ought to find it less hard to rate their stock ideas and stock phrases, their claptrap and their catchwords at their proper value, and to cast in our lot boldly with the sages and with the saints."[1] Arnold preached this doctrine indefatigably to mid-Victorian England, and he was in an exceptionally favourable position to influence educational policy, since for thirty-five years he was an official of the Education Department, and was appointed again and again as assistant to the royal commissioners that were appointed to consider educational policy. Yet I do not think it can be said that his influence was great on the thing that mattered most and on which he was most right—namely, the spiritual foundation of culture. Not only so, but he was himself in part responsible for the general unpopularity and bad odour into which the idea of culture has fallen in this country. For Matthew Arnold was what is now known as a highbrow. He was, indeed, the original and archetypal highbrow, and the war he declared against the enemies of

[1] Preface to *Irish Essays* (1882).

culture was ultimately followed by that reaction against culture and that Philistine reign of terror under which we live to-day.

The fact is that culture by itself—even a humanist culture that is intellectually aware of the spiritual values of Christianity—does not possess the power of restoring or transforming the life of society. It provides standards of value, intellectual and aesthetic appreciation, the development of the power of criticism, width of knowledge, and detachment from the prejudice and errors both of the multitude and of the ruling class. All this Arnold had—like his contemporaries Renan and Saint-Beuve in France, or Emerson and Henry James and Henry Adams in America, all of them superior people who stood aside on their intellectual eminence and watched the stream of life go by. They none of them had the religious attitude to life, though they all realized how important it was to have it. They lacked faith, and therefore they lacked charity, and therefore they failed to gain men's sympathies, and even aroused conscious or unconscious antagonism.

This is why the Utilitarians, the apostles of useful knowledge and applied science, have been their superiors in the educational field, though their views were often so much more narrow and superficial. They had a simple naïve faith in the value of concrete objective knowledge which they communicated to others. And this created a bond of sympathy between Utilitarian highbrows like Bentham and Mill and hardheaded practical men like Francis Place.

In the past, in a Christian society, the leaders of culture were just as critical of the views and behaviour of common humanity as were the modern humanists. But even the most highbrow of Christian teachers such as Pascal and Newman stood on common ground with the common people before the supreme mystery of faith.

> "God of Abraham, God of Isaac, God of Jacob,
> Not of the philosophers and men of learning,
>   God of Jesus Christ,
> Deum meum et Deum vestrum."

The mystery of faith brings all men together at the heart of life, and it reduces the differences of culture, in the humanist sense of the word, to comparative insignificance.

Faith is therefore the beginning and end of Christian culture, as it is the beginning and end of Christian morals. This is common to all forms of Christianity, Catholic, Orthodox and Protestant; only in so far as the conception of faith differs is there also a difference in the conception of culture. Indeed, I do not think it is too far-fetched to suggest that the essential difference between the Catholic and Protestant conceptions of the relation of religion and culture is bound up with their respective conceptions of the relation of faith and works; the famous controversy which above all others divided the Churches at the Reformation. For just as Catholics taught that there was a vital organic inseparable relation between faith and works, as against the Protestant view of justification by faith alone, so too in the Catholic view there is an organic relation between religion and culture, which the Protestant view does not as a rule recognize. And this, I think, is one of the main causes for that indifference of modern Protestantism to culture which was the burden of Matthew Arnold's controversial writings—the grimness and greyness of certain aspects of English and American life in the nineteenth century and the indifference of the most religious sections of English and American society to the cause of higher education.

To-day this is a thing of the past. The harsh and ugly sub-culture of Victorian industrialism, with its combination of unlimited acquisitiveness with narrow pietism, has no defenders, and the reaction against Puritanism has carried England and America to the opposite extreme of an extroverted hedonistic mass culture. But some things have been carried over from one extreme to the other without much change, and the most important of these are the contempt for ideas and the indifference to humane culture which are hardly less characteristic of the mass-man of to-day than of the individualistic Philistine of yesterday. The latter, even though they were themselves men of genuine religious faith and moral earnestness, were the destroyers of the Christian tradition of culture, and their successors have filled the void with a materialist pseudo-culture which is the real opium of the people, since it is at once a drug and an intoxicant and a poison.

For modern civilization to-day seems to be following the same road as the ancient world under the Roman Empire. On the one hand, a vast development of material resources and luxury—above all, luxury for the masses—bread and games and baths and theatres; on the other, the vast development of power—the overwhelming pressure of unlimited power, concentrated in the hands of the masters of the world. But in our case the danger is greater, because our power and resources are incomparably greater and because the tradition we are losing is not that of the pagan city-state, but that of Christendom. Nevertheless, this gloomy parallel is not altogether a hopeless one. For the decline of the classical culture and the growth of the massive power of world-state did not actually produce in the long run a materialist culture. They were followed by a sudden escape of humanity into a new spiritual dimension, the discovery of a new spiritual world and the acquisition of a new spiritual freedom. It was the age of Tiberius and Nero that saw the coming of Christianity, and the breakdown of the giant fabric of the world-state in the third century was followed by the rise of the new Christian culture.

The present crisis of our civilization can be solved only by a similar process of radical conversion and spiritual transformation. For, hard as it may be to see the possibility of it, it is no less difficult to believe in the possibility of definite progress along the present line to some robot Utopia. Indeed, the catastrophes of the last thirty years are not only a sign of the bankruptcy of secular humanism, they only go to show that a completely secularized civilization is inhuman in the absolute sense—hostile to human life and irreconcilable with human nature itself. For, as I have tried to explain in my recent books, especially *The Judgment of the Nations*, the forces of violence and aggressiveness that threaten to destroy our world are the direct result of the starvation and frustration of man's spiritual nature. For a time Western civilization managed to live on the moral tradition of the past maintained by a kind of sublimated humanitarian idealism. But this was essentially a transitional phenomenon, and as humanism and humanitarianism fade away, we see societies more and more animated by the blind will to power which drives them on to destroy one another and ultimately themselves. Civilization can be creative and life-giving only in the proportion that it is spiritualized. Otherwise the increase of power inevitably increases its power for evil—its destructiveness.

Therefore it is only by the re-discovery of the spiritual world and the restoration of man's spiritual capacities that it is possible to save humanity from self-destruction. This is the immense task which Christian education has to undertake. It involves a great deal more than any Christian or any educationalist has yet realized. And this is inevitable, because we are dealing with unknown factors which lie beyond our horizon of vision, below our level of consciousness, and above the capacity of our reason—in other words, the problem concerns the future, the human soul and God : three things which we cannot understand. For this reason, modern man, who has been accustomed to living in a world which is scientifically known and technologically controlled, is in a worse position for dealing with the ultimate religious problems than his ancestors, who were at every turn faced with mysterious forces over which they had no control, and who consequently felt an obvious, immediate, practical sense of dependence on the power and assistance of God.

But this does not mean that we ought to acquiesce, as some

modern Christian thinkers are inclined to do, in the complete incomprehensibility and otherness of Faith—in a dualism of religion and culture which leaves no room for Christian education. The greater is our knowledge of nature and man and history, the greater is the obligation to use these increased resources for God, not merely in the way of moral action, but intellectually also, by the reinterpretation of the tradition of Christian culture in terms of the new knowledge and by relating the instruments of culture to their true spiritual end.

At the present time there is a great danger that the part of culture should be under-valued and neglected both in the religious and the educational spheres. In the latter there is a tendency to sacrifice the humanities to science and technology; in the former there is the theological dualism to which I have just referred, which finds its most striking expression in the Barthian return to the theology of Luther and Calvin presented in a new dialectical form. Both these tendencies in their different ways are unfavourable to the traditional Christian culture and to the old discipline of studies which was conceived as an ascending scale of humanity, philosophy and divinity. The disintegration of higher education into a mass of divergent speculations co-ordinated only by motives of economic and political interest is fatal to any ideal of culture, and if, as is sometimes the case, religious knowledge is treated as one of these independent specialisms, it is even more fatal to religion. The recovery of a Christian culture is therefore the essential educational and religious task, and it is inseparable from the social ideal of Christendom—of the Christian people —*plebs Christiana—populus Dei*. This ideal, which has become so pale and remote to the individualism and secularism of the nineteenth century, and indeed of the whole modern world, lies at the very heart of Christianity. It was equally present in the Middle Ages, when Christendom was a triumphant world culture, and in the days when Christianity

was a persecuted underground movement, but when nevertheless Christians were conscious of being a new people, "a
third race" in whose hands the ends of the world had come.

If from the standpoint of the Roman man of the world
these Christians were an uneducated lot of barbarians, we
must remember that they were in reality just as much the
heirs of a tradition of culture as the cultivated Hellenist, and
that they brought into the tired and sophisticated civilization
of the Roman Empire the accumulated treasures of a profound
spiritual experience which was on a different plane of reality
from anything that Greece and Rome had known. And in the
modern world there is a similar tradition of sacred culture
which it has been the mission of the Church to nourish and
preserve. However secularized our modern civilization may
become, this sacred tradition remains like a river in the desert,
and a genuine religious education can still use it to irrigate
the thirsty lands and to change the face of the world with the
promise of a new life. The great obstacle is the failure of
Christians themselves to understand the depth of that tradition and the inexhaustible possibilities of new life it contains.

IV. TOWARDS A CHRISTIAN AESTHETIC [1]

by

DOROTHY L. SAYERS.

I AM to speak to you to-night about the Arts in this country—
their roots in Christianity, their present condition, and the
means by which (if we find that they are not flourishing as
they should) their mutilated limbs and withering branches
may be restored by re-grafting into the main trunk of Christian
tradition.

This task is of quite peculiar difficulty, and I may not be
able to carry it out in exactly the terms which have been proposed to me. And that for a rather strange reason. In such
things as politics, finance, sociology and so on, there really is a
philosophy and a Christian tradition; we do know more or less
what the Church has said and thought about them, how they
are related to Christian dogma, and what they are supposed to
do in a Christian country.

But oddly enough, we have no Christian aesthetic—no
Christian philosophy of the Arts. The Church as a body has
never made up her mind about the Arts, and it is hardly too
much to say that she has never tried. She has, of course,

---

[1] It will be immediately obvious how deeply this paper is indebted to
R. G. Collingwood's *Principles of Art*, particularly as regards the dis-
entangling of "Art Proper" (expression and imagination) from the
"pseudo-Arts" of "amusement" and "magic". The only contribution I
have made of my own (exclusive of incidental errors) has been to suggest,
however tentatively, a method of establishing the principles of "Art
Proper" upon that Trinitarian doctrine of the nature of Creative Mind
which does, I think, really underlie them. On this foundation it might
perhaps be possible to develop a Christian aesthetic which, finding its
source and sanction in the theological centre, would be at once more
characteristically Christian and of more universal application than any
aesthetic whose contact with Christianity is made only at the ethical
circumference.

from time to time puritanically denounced the Arts as irreligious and mischievous, or tried to exploit the Arts as a means to the teaching of religion and morals—but I shall hope to show you that both these attitudes are false and degrading, and are founded upon a completely mistaken idea of what Art is supposed to be and do. And there have, of course, been plenty of writers on aesthetics who happened to be Christians, but they have seldom made any consistent attempt to relate their aesthetic to the central Christian dogmas. Indeed, so far as European aesthetic is concerned, one feels that it would probably have developed along precisely the same lines had there never been an incarnation to reveal the nature of God— that is to say, the nature of all truth. But that is fantastic. If we commit ourselves to saying that the Christian revelation discovers to us the nature of *all* truth, then it must discover to us the nature of the truth about Art among other things. It is absurd to go placidly along explaining Art in terms of a pagan aesthetic, and taking no notice whatever of the complete revolution of our ideas about the nature of things that occurred, or should have occurred, after the First Pentecost. I will go so far as to maintain that the extraordinary confusion of our minds about the nature and function of Art is principally due to the fact that for nearly 2,000 years we have been trying to reconcile a pagan, or at any rate a Unitarian aesthetic with a Christian, that is a Trinitarian and Incarnational, theology. Even that makes us out too intelligent. We have not tried to reconcile them. We have merely allowed them to exist side by side in our minds; and where the conflict between them became too noisy to be overlooked, we have tried to silence the clamour by main force, either by brutally subjugating Art to religion, or by shutting them up in separate prison-cells and forbidding them to hold any communication with one another.

Now, before we go any further, I want to make it quite

clear that what I am talking about now is Aesthetic (the philosophy of Art) and not about Art itself as practised by the artists. The great artists carry on with their work on the lines God has laid down for them, quite unaffected by the aesthetic worked out for them by philosophers. Sometimes, of course, artists themselves dabble in aesthetic and what they have to say is very interesting, but often very misleading. If they really are great and true artists, they make their poem (or whatever it is) first, and then set about reconciling it with the fashionable aesthetic of their time; they do not produce their work to conform to their notions of aesthetic—or, if they do, they are so much the less artists, and the work suffers. Secondly, what artists chatter about to the world and to each other is not as a rule their art but the technique of their art. They will tell you, as critics, how it is they produce certain effects (the poet will talk about assonance, alliteration, and metre; the painter about perspective, balance, and how he mixes his colours, etc.)—and from that we may get the misleading impression that the technique *is* the art, or that the aim of art is to produce some sort of "effect". But this is not so. We cannot go for a march unless we have learnt, through long practice, how to control the muscles of our legs; but it is not true to say that the muscular control *is* the march. And while it is a fact that certain tricks produce "effects"—like Tennyson's use of vowels and consonants to produce the effect of a sleepy murmuring in, "The moan of doves in immemorial elms", or of metallic clashing in, "The bare black cliff clanged round him"—it is not true that the poem *is* merely a set of physical, or even of emotional effects. What a work of art really is and does we shall come to later. For the moment I only want to stress the difference between aesthetic and art, and to make it clear that a great artist will produce great art, even though the aesthetic of his time may be hopelessly inadequate to explain it.

For the origins of European aesthetic we shall, of course, turn to Greece ; and we are at once brought up against the two famous chapters in which Plato discusses the Arts, and decides that certain kinds of Art, and in particular certain kinds of poetry, ought to be banished from the perfect State. Not all poetry—people often talk as though Plato had said this, but he did not: certain kinds he wished to keep, and this makes his attitude all the more puzzling, because, though he tells us quite clearly why he disapproves of the rejected kinds, he never explains what it is that makes the other kinds valuable. He never gets down to considering, constructively, what true Art is or what it does. He only tells us about what are (in his opinion) the bad results of certain kinds of Art— nor does he ever tackle the question whether the bad moral results of which he complains may not be due to a falseness *in* the Art—*i.e.* to the work's being pseudo-Art or inartistic Art. He seems to say that certain forms of Art are inherently evil in themselves. His whole handling of the thing seems to us very strange, confused, and contradictory; yet his aesthetic has dominated all our critical thinking for many centuries, and has influenced, in particular, the attitude of the Church more than the Church perhaps knows. So it is necessary that we should look at Plato's argument. Many of his conclusions are true—though often, I think, he reaches them from the wrong premises. Some of them are, I think, demonstrably false. But especially, his whole grasp of the subject is inadequate. That is not Plato's fault. He was one of the greatest thinkers of all time, but he was a pagan: and I am becoming convinced that no pagan philosopher could produce an adequate aesthetic, simply for lack of a right theology. In this respect, the least in the Kingdom of Heaven is greater than John the Baptist.

What does Plato say?

He begins by talking about stories and myths, and after

dismissing as beneath consideration the stories and poems which are obviously badly written, he goes on to reject those which are untrue, or which attribute evil and disgusting behaviour to the gods, or which tend to inculcate bad and vulgar passions or anti-social behaviour in the audience. After this (which sounds very much like what moralists and clergymen are always saying nowadays) he leaves the subject-matter and goes on to certain *forms* of poetry and art—those forms which involve *mimesis*—the mimetic arts. Now *mimesis* can be translated "imitation", or "representation"; and we can at once see that certain forms of art are more mimetic than others: drama, painting and sculpture are, on the whole, mimetic—some natural object or action is represented or imitated; (though we may find exceptions in modernist and surrealist paintings which seem to represent nothing in Heaven or earth). Music, on the other hand, is not mimetic— nothing is imitated from the natural world (unless we count certain effects like the noise of drums in a martial piece, or trills and arpeggios representing the song of birds or the falling of water, down to the squeaks, brayings, twitterings and whistlings of cinema organs). In the Third Book of the *Republic*, Plato says he will allow the mimetic arts, provided that the imitation, or representation is of something morally edifying, that sets a good example; but he would banish alto-gether the representation of unworthy objects, such as national heroes wallowing about in floods of tears, and people getting drunk, or using foul language. He thinks this kind of thing bad for the actors and also for the audience. Nor (which seems odd to us) are actors to imitate anything vulgar or base, such as artisans plying their trades, galley-slaves or bos'ns; nor must there be any trivial nonsense about stage-effects and farmyard imitations. Nothing is to be acted or shown except what is worthy to be imitated, the noble actions of wise men—a gallery of good examples.

We may feel that Plato's theatre would be rather on the austere side. But in the Tenth Book he hardens his heart still further. He decides to banish *all* mimetic art—all representation of every kind; and that for two reasons.

The first reason is that imitation is a kind of cheat. An artist who knows nothing about carpentering may yet paint a carpenter so that if the picture is set up at a distance, children and stupid people may be deceived into thinking that it really is a carpenter. Moreover, in any case, the realities of things exist only in Heaven in an ideal and archetypal form; the visible world is only a pale reflection or bad imitation of the heavenly realities; and the work of art is only a cheating imitation of the visible world: therefore representational art is merely an imitation of an imitation—a deceptive trick which tickles and entertains while turning men's minds away from the contemplation of the eternal realities.

At this point some of you will begin to fidget and say "Hi! Stop! Surely there is a difference between mimicry intended to deceive and representation. I admit that there are such things as tin biscuit-boxes got up to look like the works of Charles Dickens, which may deceive the unwary, and that very simple-minded people in theatres have been known to hiss the villain or leap on the stage to rescue the heroine—but as a rule we know perfectly well that the imitation is only imitation, and not meant to take any one in. And surely there's a difference between farmyard imitations and John Gielgud playing Hamlet. And besides—even if you get an exact representation of something—say a documentary film about a war, or an exact verbal reproduction of a scene at the Old Bailey—that's not the same thing as *Coriolanus* or the trial scene in *The Merchant of Venice*; the work of art has something different, something more—poetry or a sort of a something . . ." and here you will begin to wave your hands about vaguely.

You are, of course, perfectly right. But let us for the moment just make a note of how Plato's conception of art is influenced by his theology—the visible world imitating, copying, reflecting a world of eternal changeless forms already existent elsewhere; and the artist, conceived of as a sort of craftsman or artisan engaged in *copying* or imitating something which exists already in the visible world.

Now let us take his second reason for banishing all representational art. He says that even where the action represented is in itself good and noble, the effect on the audience is bad, because it leads them to dissipate the emotions and energies that ought to be used for tackling the problems of life. The feelings of courage, resolution, pity, indignation and so on are worked up in the spectators by the mimic passions on the stage (or in pictures or music) and then frittered away in a debauch of emotion over these unreal shadows, leaving the mind empty and slack, with no appetite except for fresh sensations of an equally artificial sort.

Now, that is a real indictment against a particular kind of art, which we ought to take seriously. In the jargon of modern psychology, Plato is saying that art of this kind leads to phantasy and day-dreaming. Aristotle, coming about fifty years after Plato, defended this kind of art: he said that undesirable passions, such as pity and terror, were in this way *sublimated*—you worked them off in the theatre, where they could do no harm. If, he means, you feel an inner urge to murder your wife, you go and see *Othello* or read a good, gory thriller, and satisfy your blood-lust that way; and if we had the last part of his *Poetics*, which dealt with comedy, we should probably find it suggested, in the same way, that an excess of sexual emotion can be worked off by going to a good, dirty farce or vulgar music-hall, and blowing the whole thing away in a loud, bawdy laugh.

Now, people still argue as to whether Plato or Aristotle was right about this. But there are one or two things I want you to notice. The first is that what Plato is really concerned to banish from his perfect state is the kind of art which aims at mere entertainment—the art that dissipates energy instead of directing it into some useful channel. And though Aristotle defends "art for entertainment," it is still the same kind of art he is thinking about.

The second thing is that both Plato and Aristotle—but especially Plato—are concerned with the moral effect of art. Plato would allow representational art so long as he thought that it had the effect of canalizing the energies and directing them to virtuous action—he only banishes it, on further consideration, because he has come to the conclusion that *no* representational art of any kind—not even the loftiest tragedy—is successful in bracing the moral constitution. He does not tell us very clearly what poetry he will keep, or why, except that it is to be of what we should call a lyrical kind, and presumably, bracing and tonic in sentiment, and directly inculcating the love of the good, the beautiful and the true.

Thirdly: Plato lived at the beginning, and Aristotle in the middle of the era which saw the collapse and corruption of the great Greek civilization. Plato sees the rot setting in, and cries out like a prophet to his people to repent while there is yet time. He sees that the theatre audience is in fact looking to the theatre for nothing but amusement and entertainment, that their energies are, in fact, frittering themselves away in spurious emotion—sob-stuff and sensation, and senseless laughter, fantasy and day-dreaming, and admiration for the merely smart and slick and clever and amusing. And there is an ominous likeness between his age and ours. We too have audiences and critics and newspapers assessing every play and book and novel in terms of its "entertainment-value", and

E

a whole generation of young men and women who dream over novels and wallow in day-dreaming at the cinema, and who seemed to be in a fair way of doping themselves into complete irresponsibility over the conduct of life until war came, as it did to Greece, to jerk them back to reality. Greek civilization was destroyed; ours is not yet destroyed. But it may be well to remember Plato's warning: "If you receive the pleasure-seasoned Muse, pleasure and pain will be kings in your city instead of law and agreed principles."

And there is something else in Plato that seems to strike a familiar note. We seem to know the voice that urges artists to produce works of art "with a high moral tone"—propaganda works, directed to improving young people's minds and rousing them to a sense of their duties, "doing them good", in fact. And at the same time, we find—among artists and critics alike—a tendency to repudiate representational art, in favour of something more austere, primitive and symbolic, as though the trouble lay *there*.

It is as though, in the decline of Greece, and in what is known as the "Decline of the West", both Plato and we agreed in finding something wrong with the arts—a kind of mutual infection, by which the slick, sentimental, hedonistic art corrupts its audience, and the pleasure-loving, emotional audience in turn corrupts the arts by demanding of them nothing but entertainment-value. And the same sort of remedy is proposed in both cases—first, to get rid of "representationalism"—which, it is hoped, will take away the pleasure and entertainment and so cure the audience's itch for amusement; secondly, to concentrate on works which provide a direct stimulus to right thinking and right action.

What we have really got here is a sort of division of art into two kinds: *Entertainment—Art*, which dissipates the energies of the audience and pours them down the drain; and another kind of art which canalises energy into a sort of mill-stream to turn the wheel of action—and this we may perhaps call *Spell-binding Art.* But do these two functions comprise the whole of Art? Or are they Art at all? Are they perhaps only accidental effects of Art, or false Art—something masquerading under the name of Art—or menial tasks to which we enslave Art? Is the real nature and end of Art something quite different from either? Is the real trouble something wrong with our aesthetic, so that we do not know what we ought to look for in Art, or how to recognize it when we see it, or how to distinguish the real thing from the spurious imitation?

Suppose we turn from Plato to the actual poets he was writing about—to Aeschylus, for instance, the great writer of tragedies. Drama, certainly, is a representational art, and therefore, according to Plato, pleasure-art, entertainment-art, emotional and relaxing art, sensational art. Let us read the *Agamemnon.* Certainly it is the representation by actors of something—and of something pretty sensational; the murder of a husband by an adulterous wife. But it is scarcely sensational entertainment in the sense that a thriller-novel on the same subject is sensational entertainment. A day-dreaming, pleasure-loving audience would hardly call it entertainment at all. It is certainly not relaxing. And I doubt whether it either dissipates our passions in Plato's sense or sublimates them in Aristotle's sense, any more than it canalizes them for any particular action, though it may trouble and stir us and plunge us into the mystery of things. We might extract some moral lessons from it; but if we ask ourselves whether the poet wrote that play in order to improve our minds, something inside us will, I think, say "No". Aeschylus was trying to tell us something, but nothing quite so simple as that. He is saying something—something important—something enormous—And here we shall be suddenly struck with the inade-

quacy of the strictures against " representational art".
"This," we shall say, "is not the copy or imitation of something bigger and more real than itself. It is bigger and more
real than the real-life action that it represents. That a false
wife should murder a husband—that might be a paragraph
in the *News of the World* or a thriller to read in the train—
but when it is shown us like this, by a great poet, it is as
though we went behind the triviality of the actual event to
the cosmic significance behind it. And, what is more, this is
not a representation of the actual event at all—if a B.B.C.
reporter had been present at the murder with a television set
and microphone, what we heard and saw would have been
nothing like this. This play is not anything that ever
happened in this world—it is something happening in the
mind of Aeschylus, and it had never happened before."

Now here, I believe, we are getting to something—something that Plato's heathen philosophy was not adequate to
explain, but which we can begin to explain by the light of
Christian theology. Very likely the heathen poet could not
have explained it either—if he had made the attempt, he too
would have been entangled in the terms of his philosophy.
But we are concerned, not with what he might have said,
but with what he did. Being a true poet, he was true in his
work—that is, his art was that point of truth in him which
was true to the eternal truth, and only to be interpreted in
terms of eternal truth.

The true work of art, then, is something *new*—it is not
primarily the copy or representation of anything. It may
involve representation, but that is not what makes it a work
of art. It is not manufactured to specification, as an engineer
works to a plan—though it may involve compliance with the
accepted rules for dramatic presentation, and may also con-
tain verbal "effects" which can be mechanically accounted for.
We know very well, when we compare it with so-called

works of art which *are* "turned out to pattern" that in this connection neither circumcision availeth anything nor uncircumcision, but a new creature. Something has been created.

This word—this idea of art as *creation*—is, I believe, the one important contribution that Christianity has made to aesthetics. Unfortunately, we are apt to use the words "creation" and "creativeness" very vaguely and loosely, because we do not relate them properly to our theology. But it is significant that the Greeks had not this word in their aesthetic at all. They looked on a work of art as a kind of *techné*, a manufacture. Neither, for that matter, was the word in their theology—they did not look on history as the continual act of God fulfilling itself in creation.

How do we say that God creates? And how does this compare with the act of creation by an artist? To begin with, of course, we say that God created the universe "out of nothing"—He was bound by no conditions of any kind. Here there can be no comparison: the human artist is *in* the universe and bound by its conditions. He can create only within that framework and out of that material which the universe supplies. Admitting that, let us ask in what way God creates. Christian theology replies that God, who is a Trinity, creates by, or through, his second Person, his Word or Son, who is continually begotten from the First Person, the Father, in an eternal creative activity. And certain theologians have added this very significant comment: the Father, they say, is only known to himself by beholding his image in his Son.

Does that sound very mysterious? We will come back to the human artist, and see what it means in terms of *his* activity. But first, let us take note of a new word that has crept into the argument by way of Christian theology—the word *Image*. Suppose, having rejected the words, "copy", "imitation" and "representation" as inadequate we substitute the word "image" and say that what the artist is doing is *to image forth* something or the other, and connect that with St. Paul's phrase: "God . . . hath spoken to us by his Son, the brightness of his glory and *express image* of his person".— Something which, by being an image, *expresses* that which it images. Is that getting us a little nearer to something? There is something which is, in the deepest sense of the words, *unimaginable*, known to itself (and still more, to us) only by the image in which it expresses itself through creation; and, says Christian theology very emphatically, the Son, who is the express image, is not the copy, or imitation, or representation of the Father, nor yet inferior or subsequent to the Father in any way—in the last resort, in the depths of their mysterious being, the Unimaginable and the Image are *one and the same.*

Now for our poet. We said, when we were talking of the *Agamemnon*, that this work of art seemed to be "something happening in the mind of Aeschylus". We may now say, perhaps, more precisely, that the play is the *expression* of this interior happening. But *what*, exactly, was happening?

There is a school of criticism that is always trying to explain, or explain away, a man's works of art by trying to dig out the events of his life and his emotions *outside* the works themselves, and saying "these are the real Aeschylus, the real Shakespeare, of which the poems are only faint imitations". But any poet will tell you that this is the wrong way to go to work. It is the old, pagan aesthetic which explains nothing—or which explains all sorts of things about the work *except* what makes it a work of art. The poet will say: "My poem is the expression of my experience". But if you then say, "What experience?" he will say, "I can't tell you anything about it, except what I have said in the poem— the poem *is* the experience". The Son and the Father are *one*: the poet himself did not know what his experience was until he created the poem which revealed his own experience to himself.

To save confusion, let us distinguish between an *event* and an *experience*. An event is something that happens to one—but one does not necessarily experience it. To take an extreme instance: suppose you are hit on the head and get concussion and, as often happens, when you come to, you cannot remember the blow. The blow on the head certainly happened to you, but you did not *experience* it—all you experience is the after-effects. You only experience a thing when you can express it—however haltingly—to your own mind. You may remember the young man in T. S. Eliot's play *The Family Reunion*, who says to his relations:

> You are all people
> To whom nothing has happened, at most a continual impact
> Of external events—

He means that they have got through life without ever really *experiencing* anything, because they have never tried to express to themselves the real nature of what has happened to them.

A poet is a man who not only suffers "the impact of external events" but experiences them. He puts the experience into words in his own mind, and in so doing recognizes the experience for what it is. To the extent that we can do that, we are all poets. A "poet" so-called is simply a man like ourselves with an exceptional power of revealing his experience by expressing it, so that not only he, but we ourselves, recognize that experience as our own.

I want to stress the word *recognize*. A poet does not see something—say the full moon and say: "This is a very beautiful sight—let me set about finding words for the appropriate expression of what people ought to feel about it". That is what the literary artisan does, and it means nothing. What

happens is that then, or at some time after, he finds himself
saying words in his head and says to himself: "Yes—that is
right. *That* is the experience the full moon was to me. I
recognize it in expressing it, and now I know what it was".
And so, when it is a case of mental or spiritual experience—
sin, grief, joy, sorrow, worship—the thing reveals itself to him
in words, and so becomes fully experienced for the first time.
By thus recognizing it in its expression he makes it his own—
integrates it into himself. He no longer feels himself battered
passively by the impact of external events—it is no longer
something happening *to* him, but something happening *in*
him; the reality of the event is communicated to him in
activity and power. So that the act of the poet in creation is
seen to be threefold—a trinity—experience, expression and
recognition; the unknowable reality in the experience: the
image of that reality known in its expression: and power in the
recognition; the whole making up the single and indivisible
act of creative mind.

Now, what the poet does for himself, he can also do for us.
When he has imaged forth his experience he can incarnate it,
so to speak, in a material body—words, music, painting—the
thing we know as a work of art. And since he is a man like
the rest of us, we shall expect that our experience will have
something in common with his. In the image of *his* experience, we can *recognize* the image of some experience of our
own—something that had happened to us, but which we had
never understood, never formulated or expressed to ourselves,
and therefore never known as a real experience. When we
read the poem, or see the play or picture or hear the music,
it is as though a light were turned on inside us. We say:
"Ah! I recognize that! That is something which I obscurely
felt to be going on in and about me, but I didn't know what
it was and couldn't express it. But now that the artist has
made its image—imaged it forth—for me, I can possess and

take hold of it and make it my own, and turn it into a source of knowledge and strength." This is the *communication of the image in power*, by which the third person of the poet's trinity brings us, through the incarnate image, unto direct knowledge of the in-itself unknowable and unimaginable reality. "No man cometh to the Father save by me," said the incarnate Image; and He added, "but the Spirit of Power will lead you into all truth."

This recognition of the truth that we get in the artist's work comes to us as a revelation of new truth. I want to be clear about that. I am not referring to the sort of patronizing recognition we give to a writer by nodding our heads and observing: "Yes, yes, very good, very true—that's just what I'm always saying." I mean the recognition of a truth which tells us something about ourselves that we had *not* been "always saying"—something which puts a new knowledge of ourselves within our grasp. It is new, startling and perhaps shattering—and yet it comes to us with a sense of familiarity. We did not know it before, but the moment the poet has shown it to us, we know that, somehow or other, we had always really known it.

Very well. But, frankly, is that the sort of thing the average British citizen gets, or expects to get, when he goes to the theatre or reads a book? No, it is not. In the majority of cases, it is not in the least what he expects, or what he wants. What he looks for is not this creative and Christian kind of Art at all. He does not expect or desire to be upset by sudden revelations about himself and the universe. Like the people of Plato's decadent Athens he has forgotten or repudiated the religious origins of all Art. He wants entertainment, or, if he is a little more serious-minded, he wants something with a moral, or to have some spell or incantation put on him to instigate him into virtuous action.

Now entertainment and moral spell-binding have their

uses, but they are not Art in the proper sense. They may be the incidental effects of good art; but they may also be the very aim and essence of false art. And if we continue to demand of the Arts only these two things, we shall starve and silence the true artist and encourage in his place the false artist, who may become a very sinister force indeed.

Let us take the amusement-art: what does that give us? Generally speaking, what we demand and get from it is the enjoyment of the emotions which usually accompany experience without having had the experience. It does not reveal us to ourselves: it merely projects on to a mental screen a picture of ourselves as we already fancy ourselves to be—only bigger and brighter. The manufacturer of this kind of entertainment is not by any means interpreting and revealing his own experience to himself and us—he is either indulging his own day-dreams, or—still more falsely and venially—he is saying: "What is it the audience think they would like to have experienced? Let us show them that, so that they can wallow in emotion by pretending to have experienced it." This kind of pseudo-art is "wish-fulfilment" or "escape" literature in the worst sense—it is an escape, not from the "impact of external events" into the citadel of experienced reality, but an escape from reality and experience into a world of merely external events—the progressive externalization of consciousness. For occasional relaxation this is all right; but it can be carried to the point where, not merely art, but the whole universe of phenomena becomes a screen on which we see the magnified projection of our unreal selves, as the object of equally unreal emotions. This brings about the complete corruption of the consciousness, which can no longer recognize reality in experience.[1] When things come

---

[1] This, in terms of Art, is the "sin against the Holy Ghost", which can know neither repentance nor forgiveness, because the very organ by which we repent and accept forgiveness is itself corrupted and impotent.

to this pass, we have a civilization which "lives for amusement"—a civilization without guts, without experience, and
out of touch with reality.

Or take the spell-binding kind of art. This at first sight
seems better because it spurs us to action: and it also has its
uses. But it too is dangerous in excess, because once again,
it does not reveal reality in experience, but only projects
a lying picture of the self. As the amusement-art seeks to
produce the *emotions* without the experience, so *this* pseudo-
art seeks to produce the *behaviour* without the experience. In
the end it is directed to putting the behaviour of the audience
beneath the will of the spell-binder, and its true name is not
"art" but "art-magic". In its vulgarest form it becomes pure
propaganda. It can (as we have reason to know) actually
succeed in making its audience into the thing it desires to
have them—it can really in the end corrupt the consciousness
and destroy experience until the inner selves of its victims are
wholly externalized and made the puppets and instruments
of their own spurious passions. This is why it is dangerous
for anybody—even for the Church—to urge artists to produce works of art for the express purpose of "doing good to
people". Let her by all means encourage artists to express
their own Christian experience and communicate it to others.
That is the true artist saying: "Look! recognize your experience in my own." But "edifying art" may only too often be
the pseudo-artist corruptly saying: "This is what you are
supposed to believe and feel and do—and I propose to work
you into a state of mind in which you will believe and feel
and do as you are told." This pseudo-art does not really
communicate power to us; it merely exerts power over us.

What is it, then, that these two pseudo-arts—the enter-
taining and the spell-binding—have in common? And how
are they related to true Art? What they have in common is
the falsification of the consciousness; and they are to Art as

the *idol* is to the Image. The Jews were forbidden to make
any image for worship, because before the revelation of the
threefold unity in which Image and Unimaginable are one, it
was only too fatally easy to substitute the idol for the Image.
The Christian revelation set free all the images, by showing
that the true Image subsisted within the Godhead Itself—it
was neither copy, nor imitation, nor representation, nor
inferior nor subsequent, but the brightness of the glory, and
the express image of the Person—the very mirror in which
reality knows itself and communicates itself in power.

But the danger still exists; and it always will recur whenever
the Christian doctrine of the Image is forgotten. In our
aesthetic, that doctrine has never been fully used or understood, and in consequence our whole attitude to the artistic
expression of reality has become confused, idolatrous and
pagan. We see the Arts degenerating into mere entertainment
which corrupts and relaxes our civilization, and we try in
alarm to correct this by demanding a more moralizing and
bracing kind of Art. But this is only setting up one idol in
place of the other. Or we see that Art is becoming idolatrous,
and suppose that we can put matters right by getting rid of
the representational element in it. But what is wrong is not
the representation itself, but the fact that what we are looking
at, and what we are looking *for*, is not the Image but an idol.
Little children, keep yourselves from idols.

It has become a commonplace to say that the Arts are in a
bad way. We are in fact largely given over to the entertainers
and the spell-binders; and because we do not understand that
these two functions do not represent the true nature of Art,
the true artists are, as it were, excommunicate, and have no
audience. But there is here not, I think, so much a relapse
from a Christian aesthetic as a failure ever to find and examine
a real Christian aesthetic, based on dogma and not on ethics.
This may not be a bad thing. We have at least a new line of

country to explore, that has not been trampled on and built over and fought over by countless generations of quarrelsome critics. What we have to start from is the Trinitarian doctrine of creative mind, and the light which that doctrine throws on the true nature of images.

The great thing, I am sure, is not to be nervous about God —not to try and shut out the Lord Immanuel from *any* sphere of truth. Art is not He—we must not substitute Art for God; yet this also is He, for it is one of His Images and therefore reveals His nature. Here we see in a mirror darkly— we behold only the images; elsewhere we shall see face to face, in the place where Image and Reality are one.

V. WORK AND THE CRISIS OF OUR CULTURE

by

Maurice B. Reckitt

"I LIKE work: it fascinates me. I can sit and look at it for hours. I love to keep it by me: the idea of getting rid of it nearly breaks my heart."[1] It is obvious that the author of these words, who made no bones about describing himself as an "Idle Fellow", is not referring to that joy at watching others work which guarantees that any trio of labourers making a hole in a London street will not be without an audience impressed and even fascinated, if not by their skill at any rate by their energy. The work that he "can sit and look at for hours" is the work he himself has got to do, the work he is going to do—but not going to do just yet. Not many of the world's workers perhaps are in a position to afford themselves this subtle joy. The worker on the "assembly line" who loved to keep his work by him would not find himself loved by the scientific manager; the factory hand, reluctant to get rid of his task, might not find his employer reluctant to get rid of him. (Yet even here there is a doubt, and cases are not unknown where contracts into which a time basis enters have been prolonged by co-operation between employer and employed.) The paradox of at once loving the idea of work and not particularly loving the doing of it is, however, something more subtle than a mere joke. For we all tend to be influenced in some degree by two ideas about Work without for the most part being aware of any contradiction, or at any rate tension between them. Work is

[1] *Three Men in a Boat*, by Jerome K. Jerome, Chapter 15.

a curse and a burden of which man never ceases to complain and of which he is always trying to relieve himself by the devising of "labour-saving" appliances of one sort or another. Work imprisons us by its routine, and maims our nature by denying to us the spontaneity of leisure, the refreshment of beauty and the dignity of contemplation. Even men happy in their work and satisfied as to its value feel this at times. They ask with Lamb:

> Who first invented Work—and tied the free
> And holy-day rejoicing spirit down
> To the ever-haunting importunity
> Of business in the green fields and the town?

and those perhaps ask it most often who find themselves enslaved to what he calls

> this dry drudgery of the desk's dead wood.

"Life wastes itself while we are preparing to live," and for many it chiefly seems to waste itself in work.

But there is another view of Work, an idea often basely exploited and degraded by those interested in commending assiduity to others, but an idea nevertheless which most of us feel to be authentic and often find to be spontaneous. Work is the activity by which man holds his lawful tenure upon earth; its faithful performance is his pre-eminent, perhaps his sole, title to honour and—as many would (I think mistakenly) argue—to remuneration. We often find it difficult to give anyone higher praise than to say of him that he "does his job". And it is now a commonplace that the worst hardship suffered by the unemployed man is a conscious loss of social significance. When he has lost his job he has lost his status, and he begins to fear that he will lose his soul.

It is, or at any rate it ought to be, obvious that this almost universal intuition that Work is at once a curse and a blessing is something which, while it may belong to the perennial consciousness of man, at any rate in Europe, has been con-

siderably influenced and, I think, perverted by the technological developments of the last two hundred years, as also
by certain ideological ones which antedated them and have
largely determined the use to which they have been put. I
propose to say more about this in a moment, but it is clear
that the sort of curse which Work has become to millions
• since the dawn of the Industrial Revolution is a curse quite
different from any experienced before, either in Christian
history or in the simpler economies of primitive societies, a
curse comparable, and then only in certain limited respects,
to the organized slave labour of the great pagan civilizations.
And again, the peculiar prestige attached to economic routine,
whether in the form of business by the moralists of the
Puritan tradition, or as mass-production by the Marxian,
with his glorification of "the worker" whose triumph is to
usher in a new millennial age—this prestige is something
quite fresh in history. These accentuations of the curse and
the blessing men have felt to be indissolubly connected in
work are something unhealthy and abnormal; they represent
that sort of hypertrophy of truth which becomes untruthful,
something so much larger than life that it ceases to be life-
like. The exaggeration is so gross that we cannot perceive the
reality which it conceals. We have to step back a little to get
a truer view. We shall perhaps do well to step back a good
long way—as far, in fact, as the Garden of Eden.

The two accounts which we have of man as pictured
before the Fall agree in this—that he is not to be only a
spectator of creation; he is to be a co-operator with it. He
was put into the Garden, says the earlier account, "to dress it
and to keep it"; he is to "replenish the earth and subdue it",
says the later one. Work, then, in the Biblical view of life, is
not essentially a curse; man was called to be active even in his
innocence. It has been well pointed out in a French Catholic
essay towards a Christian philosophy of work that

"God has not made of nature merely a spectacle to be gazed at and imitated. . . . The Christian universe (in distinction from the Greek disposition to look upon the world as a *cosmos*) is handed over to man, in order that he may make it worthier of God. It is not complete and does not rejoice in a perfection which is static and immutable. . . . The worker is first of all the gardener who pushes back from his grassy prairie the virgin forest, the vegetable anarchy which is a constant menace and would, were it not for his laborious effort, soon be the victor in the struggle. He does more; he gives the human note to the landscape, or rather, he creates the landscape, roads, agriculture and cities. . . . Nature without man is less divine than nature with man, since there is lacking in it his meaning and his accomplishment. Work is that natural redemption which humanizes the world and makes man divine."

Hence, to be a worker

is a metaphysical dignity which gives to the humble activity of the muscles the rank of a secondary cause and makes them collaborator in the development of creation.[1]

Thus man in the intention of his Creator is raised above the level of the animals and made responsible for providing for himself. And for providing, be it noted, not only for his needs, but for all those "plus values" which instinct by itself does not produce. That there is a certain effort demanded from man to overcome the inertia which is part of his fallen nature is no doubt true; this represents that "penal" element implied in the declaration that "in the sweat of thy brow shalt thou eat bread". But this element of strain has never been inconsistent with, or even hostile to, that other element of satisfaction which comes to many a craftsman in the process of work, and to many more who have perhaps found a process toilsome, but are rewarded at the end by the contemplation of a task well done. It is very important that there should be no confusion between the moral and physical strain exacted

[1] *A Philosophy of Work*, by E. Borne and F. Henry (1938), pp. 119–121.

F

from man as a condition of the just satisfaction of his needs, which is the inherited consequence of original sin, and the many inhuman disabilities imposed upon workers by their fellows, which are the direct or historical consequences of actual sin. The curse of Adam is one thing; the curse of Adam Smith (if I may summarize in a single name the tyrannical fallacies of modern economics) quite another.

There is no need to explore once again the significance of our Lord's choice to be born not into a family of priests or scribes, but into what was in the most direct and simple sense a workman's home.[1] The village carpenter is perhaps pre-eminently the village craftsman. His occupation, more than that of most men, tends to unite utility to creativeness, and thus to express in simplest form the two elements which should ever make themselves manifest in work. It has often been remarked how commonly the material of Christ's parables is drawn from the normal activities of the countryside. It is perhaps worth noting, too, that while the call to many of his first disciples does not, at any rate in the early days, involve their withdrawal from the avocations by the lakeside by which the natural needs of man are supplied, when the call to that apostle who was implicated in the artificial world of financial transactions is made, it does seem to imply Matthew's retirement from his worldly business. Our Lord does not call his apostles into a monastery; he accepts the world of work into which he and they were born as capable of being the medium for the sort of fellowship into which he was calling them, for all that the vast missionary enterprise to which they would ultimately be led would inevitably create for them an entirely new vocation. But while Christ

---

[1] This paragraph and the five which follow it are reproduced from my book *Religion in Social Action* (published in 1937). As this volume has been for seven years out of print I feel justified in transcribing these passages, and thus avoiding a laborious paraphrase of the matter therein dealt with.

thus accepts this natural economy, by implied contrast, it would seem, with the purely acquisitive operations of the plutocracy which we know to have reached a highly developed stage in the Palestine of his day, two conditions of that acceptance have to be borne in mind. First, the production that our Lord accepts is essentially "on account of man"[1] and not on account of gain. The gospels are permeated through and through with warnings as to the perils of accepting mere personal acquisition as the purpose of human activity. And secondly, nowhere does Jesus exalt activity at the expense of that more profound aspect of life which is often expressed by the term "contemplation". His emphasis is, indeed, all in the other direction.

The Church of the first three centuries, while on the whole it exhibited in the economic, as in so many other spheres, the characteristics of the fellowship it so pre-eminently strove to be, does not offer much of significance for our present purpose for two reasons. First, because its attitude of expectation of an early second coming of its Lord militated against any concern with the social organization of a world order destined at any moment to pass away. And secondly, because it had in any case no power to influence the secular authorities of an empire in which it was a despised and often a persecuted minority. Too much should not be made of the "voluntary communism" of the earliest days; suggestive though it is of the order of values established in the hearts of the first believers, it is significant rather as a spiritual attitude than as a social expedient. Still less ought to be built upon the famous observation of St. Paul that he who will not work neither shall he eat. Though it may be going too far to describe this as a "casual dictum", as one commentator has done, in reaction against the exaggerated effort to build up a

---

[1] "Production is on account of man, not man of production." St. Antonino of Florence.

social philosophy upon a single text, it is certainly unjusti-
fiable to employ this admonition as the sanction for an
authoritarian compulsion to work for all in all circumstances
for all time. St. Paul is merely saying that in a simple
economy, where the services of all are needed for the support
of all, those services can rightly be claimed in the common
interest. Translated into contemporary phraseology, this text
merely exhorts us to "pull our weight".

St. Paul's observation, however, was certainly not at
variance with the Christian doctrine of work as it came to be
formed in those "ages of faith" during which economic theory
and practice developed under the direct influence of religion.
And this is entirely natural, since for a thousand years and
more after the apostle wrote, the human economy was one
which demanded the labour of all if the traditional standards
of living were not to fall. The medieval period was still what
a rather misleading modern phrase describes as an "age of
scarcity", and in such circumstances it was but natural that
work should present itself to the social philosopher as something designed by Providence to furnish at once a discipline
for the individual and a service to society.[1] But it must be
appreciated that such work was neither "work for work's
sake" nor a relentless pursuit of gain. Medieval work was
essentially "on account of man", both as maker and user. It
was almost invariably done in community, even on the land,
in what was, however defectively, the community of the
manor. It was normally the work of one not without proprietorship of his own, or good hope of attaining it. It was
work done to a natural rhythm, and in being so far less
psychologically exacting than are the great majority of
occupations to-day. And it was work constantly interrupted

[1] No doubt the "penal" element, held to be implicit in the Fall, was
disproportionately emphasized by many medieval teachers. But by
contrast with the outlook of the pagan philosophers the work of the ordinary man was accepted as a mode of the good life.

by holidays, which were, of course, "holy days", holidays so numerous as gravely to shock the solemn-faced economists of a relentless industrialism, who have always been contemptuous of a period which did not accord to the process of accumulation the primacy which post-Reformation philosophers have always freely conceded.

Now, it is extremely important to recall the conditions amid which this universal obligation to work was fulfilled, because efforts have been made in succeeding ages, and are being made still, to apply this Christian sanction for work to a set of entirely different social circumstances. That a medieval cobbler should work with his own tools to supply the needs of his neighbours, and thus get his own living without becoming a burden upon them, is one thing, and few or none will think it an unreasonable thing. But that a modern proletarian boot operative should be required to labour for eight or more hours a day in a boot factory, year in, year out, for the profit of an international combine, is quite another thing; and it is (or ought to be) very far from being obvious that the same sanctions of Christian duty and social obligation can be applied to the two situations. The economic developments of the last two hundred years have brought about two vast revolutions: that which confirmed the status of the mass of the population as one of proletarian dependence on a class made suddenly rich by the new machines of the steam age, and that which has brought into being the "world of plenty", in which, largely through the operation of electric power, the necessity and the practicability of exacting labour service from every member of the community is, to put it moderately, no longer a self-evident truth.

In such circumstances it should be obvious that we need a restatement of Christian teaching about the relation of man to his work and his livelihood. For Christian thought is still under the influence, not indeed of medieval standards in

these matters, but of the distortion to which those standards
were subjected in the post-Reformation period. As a result
of this distortion, economic activity became detached, both in
idea and fact, from any relation to its social justification and
purpose, and from any control by moral forces (such as
those which operated through the medieval guilds) over its
methods. Work, for whatever end and of whatever kind,
came to be conceived of as constituting man's duty before
all else, and since it was thus blessed, clearly the more there
was of it the better.[1] Economic activity, indeed, became
accepted as a sort of guarantee of moral integrity. Not
unnaturally, on such an assumption, profits began to be
regarded as a measure of personal and social rectitude; not
only the merited, but almost the automatic reward of a wor-
shipful energy.[2] Profits, however, it presently appeared,
were increasingly for the few, and this for two reasons.
Partly owing to the still too little appreciated fact that the
flair for profit-making is a particular talent among many other
human capacities, and not a universal attribute, forfeited only
by the indolent. The "typical business man" is a special
kind of man among many other kinds of men, who also contribute in their different ways to the prosperity and happiness
of society. But the further and more immediately decisive
reason why profits were for the few was that the developments in technique, which culminated in the Industrial Revolution, made a widely distributed ownership a steadily
diminishing social phenomenon. Proprietorship of any kind
began to be the exception. But economic assiduity was the
duty of all. Thus the new steam power and the great

[1] Moreover, as the two French Catholic sociologists already quoted
point out in their penetrating study of the subject, "work was needed to
steel the soul which rejected joy."—*A Philosophy of Work*, by E. Borne
and F. Henry, p. 61.
[2] "The accumulation of money is not a sin, since every one of the
hoarded coins represents a pleasure not to be enjoyed."—Borne and
Henry, op. cit., p. 62.

machines, when they came, found society at a stage of ideological and social development out of which plutocracy and proletarianism were bound to emerge. Not only was "man on account of production"; he was on account of a production vastly expanding at the direction and for the gain of a handful of his fellows.

The "capitalism" which began as individual enterprise, but appears to be ending as monopolistic restriction, has conferred many material benefits on mankind. But for these a heavy price has been paid in the sacrifice both of normal human relations between men and classes and of personal responsibility and freedom. Our industrial system, indeed, in its inversion of values, is the inevitable result of the philosophy of economic secularism.[1] From the horrors of employment under George III to the horrors of unemployment under George VI, it has exhibited the fatal consequences of identifying man's social significance with the fact of his economic activity. Economic secularism, from its first formulation by the sixteenth-century Puritans, has suspected spontaneity and joy and all "undisciplined" and "useless" energy. Combining a self-satisfied rectitude with a dehumanizing callousness, it was rationalized into an unsocial science by its scribes, the Victorian economists, and has culminated in the complete social irresponsibility of "Sound Finance", which is ready, with a good conscience, to mutiliate man, physically and psychologically, in order to preserve the validity of "economic laws".

Christianity to-day is confronted and challenged all along the line by a philosophy which is a consequence of the perversion of its spirit and of the social abdication of the Church.

The old religious sanctions for claiming from the in-

---

[1] But notice that "the Puritan assumption that work would always guarantee at least bread and honour belongs to a world of small masters—proletarianism shatters it".—Borne and Henry, op. cit., p. 78.

dividual that he should make a contribution to the common stock were first perverted into a justification for employing him for the purposes and profit of another: this perversion we know as the wage system. They are now being applied to suggest that man's civic status and social security must and ought to depend upon his being "fully employed" in some recognizable category, irrespective of the validity of what he is employed to do or even, it would seem, of any genuine need the production system may come to have of his full-time services. This is the employment hypothesis, some implications of which we shall have to explore. There is of course a legitimate sense in which man may be said to have what has often been claimed for him, namely, a "right to work", for if man is not afforded opportunities to occupy himself usefully, society is robbed and the individual is frustrated. But when the phrase is interpreted to mean that while a man is entitled to have a job found for him, he has got to be satisfied with any job, however futile, so long as he is adequately paid for it, a fatal confusion is introduced between subsistence and service, and between "busyness" and vocation. Man's right to work is only truly recognized when three conditions are satisfied. First, his occupation must be a *"ministry"*; one by which society will be well served if the job is well done. Secondly, his occupation must be capable of being for him a *vocation*; the worker must be able to contribute to it something which, even though not specifically his own, is at least not at war with his nature. And thirdly, the occupation, unless it happens to be a solitary task, must have about it some quality of *partnership*; the worker must share at some stage in the decisions about the arrangement of what is done, and in any legitimate profit which results from it, so that his labour is not treated as a mere cost of production.

These standards are Christian standards: they were the standards applied, in principle at any rate, by the traditional social philosophy in those ages when all economic teaching was Christian teaching. That they have been submerged since is due not only to the triumph of standards derived from other—in essence anti-Christian—sources, but to the misunderstanding by Christian people of what is primary and what is secondary in a religious attitude to secular affairs. Christians have too often been betrayed by the emotions very naturally aroused in them by contemplation of the consequences of "emancipating" economics from control by moral considerations into supposing that the industrial problem is primarily an ethical one. They have looked to remedy in the sphere of personal conduct for maladies which commonly originate in a perversion of social and individual purpose. As Miss Dorothy Sayers has declared,

> "The reason why the Churches are in so much difficulty about giving a lead in the economic sphere is because they are trying to fit a Christian standard of economics to a wholly false and pagan understanding of work."[1]

It is not the mission of the Church, as is so often declared, to "hallow" all work or to declare every man's job a "vocation". The author of a recent volume on worship has pointed out the dangerous fallacy involved here.

> "It would be wrong to assume that anything and everything can be redeemed simply by being offered or 'done as for God'. There are some things—and in the modern world many more than one would think—which are in themselves unreal, and which therefore are simply unofferable. It may be true
>
> > Who sweeps, as for thy laws,
> > Makes that and the action fine,
>
> but it is emphatically not true that he who calls at every door along a street, using every blandishment to persuade the reluctant housewife to buy a carpet sweeper or a vacuum cleaner that she does not want and cannot really afford, can ever make that and the action fine. The system which compels

[1] *Why Work?*, p. 11.

> human beings to undertake unproductive and anti-social jobs
> as the price of their own livelihood, and which yet more
> culpably inverts the whole natural order of production and
> distribution so that the primary industry, agriculture, is
> almost crushed out of existence whilst finance which is itself
> a 'no-thing' but a mere mechanism for the distribution of
> things that are real, dominates and controls the whole
> economic system in its own fictitious interests—such a system
> is incapable of redemption by the symbolic offering of iso-
> lated pieces of its product at Divine Service as a sort of sop
> to the Creator." [1]

As Miss Sayers succinctly remarks, "It is the duty of the
Church to see to it that the work serves God and that the
worker serves the work". Unless this is true of an industrial
task, that task not only fails to attain the level of a vocation:
it cannot be accepted even as a ministry. It is—or ought to
be—alarming to realize how many processes in our irrational
and meretricious industrial system fail to be either.

It is foolish to suppose that the evil implicit in such a state
of affairs can be cured by the infusion of a "new spirit". I
may put new spirit into my motor-car, which may make it run
more smoothly, and even more swiftly, but it will not prevent
it from dashing over a precipice if it is headed in that direction. It is not a new spirit but a new understanding and a new
orientation that our industry requires, and this is not an
ethical problem, save in so far as the question of how to gener-
ate sufficient moral energy to enable us to effect a new valu-
ation may be held to constitute one. It is not only a religious
problem that is involved; it is a sociological one too. As Dr.
Demant declared to the Malvern Conference : [2]

> "The English are called upon to redress one of the greatest
> historical errors of humanity, the error that economic goods
> are to be measured by trader's values. The error is the

---

[1] *The Necessity of Worship*, by Patrick McLaughlin, p. 117.
[2] *Malvern* 1941: "The Life of the Church and the Order of Society",
pp. 137-138.

domination of economic purposes by the interests of exchange and sale; or in the terms of the late Will Dyson,[1] the lordship of business man over artist man, by which he meant that social policy was formed more by the type which lives by exchanging and manipulating things and needs, than by the makers, users and enjoyers of things. . . .

"For trader man a scarcity of good things is more valuable than a plentitude of them; the exchange value of each is thereby greater. The quintessence of the trader spirit is to be seen in the financier and banker as money-lender. But trader man includes all who thrive on commissions earned solely in the *movement* of things, of labour, of money and of debts. In this category, belong not only banking, stock exchange, insurance, but also salesmanship, advertizing, most of the Press *and* the bureacracy of a modern state."

A similar thesis is the foundation of Dr. Peter Drucker's important volume which appeared here two years later, *The Future of Industrial Man.* Drucker attributes many of our social and economic troubles to the fact that we have been trying to run an industrial society on mercantile assumptions. Because the realities of industrial technics and industrial power have never been boldly faced, the problem of taming and humanizing industrialism has never been faced either. It has been assumed that good-will and a purgation of motive all round would settle the matter. But to quote Dr. Demant again:

"It is unfortunately necessary to remind even a theological audience that there are other evils than those which come from bad inter-personal motives. We are not here concerned with questions of the integrity of a certain class of man; it is the place they take in the scale of social functions that is in question."

Significant of the distorted vision from which our whole view of the performance of man's industrial activities suffers is that we talk so seldom of work and so often of employment.

[1] In his book *An Artist among the Bankers.*

By the very fact of doing so the emphasis is shifted from the essential to the incidental: instead of considering what man is occupied upon we are content if he is merely occupied. An economic system is now held to be justified primarily by the degree to which it furnishes "Full Employment". That we should have come to accept such a criterion is natural enough, since a society in which the great majority have lost all proprietorial relation to their work knows no other way of affording its members an assurance (which is also largely an illusion) of status and function than by the guarantee of a "job". Thus Full Employment is not really an economic goal at all; it is an effort to outwit the process by which a developing technology proves its technical success in eliminating human agency, an effort made because the situation of a proletarianized society left without a sufficiency of imposed tasks has been seen to produce alarming consequences. Men broken in to more than a century of industrialism, and condemned to live in enormous "conurbations", without any more education than the member of a class of perhaps sixty can pick up before he is fifteen—such men cannot live without a task being provided for them. If employment does not exist it becomes the business of society to invent it, though so far no developed industrial community has found any way of continuing to do so save by the production—and ultimately the use—of armaments.

The danger is that the present post-war situation will obscure the fact that "Full Employment" is not an authentic social objective and cannot be permanently achieved. For in that situation there is an urgent need to overtake the enormous lag in the production of genuine utilities of all kinds, and there is abundant money at market, in the form of war savings and post-war credits, to absorb all that can be produced. This provides the stimulus to a full employment, the justification for which is obvious, though even so, too blind an acceptance of mere "employment" as a social value in itself may obscure the need for the recognition of certain priorities in post-war production. The late Government White Paper on Employment Policy has happily shown evidence of recognizing that this problem exists, and it will be the first duty of the Christian community to keep public opinion up to the mark in this matter in despite of any selfish interests, plutocratic or other, which may seek to influence it in an opposite sense. For if this is not done, one or both of two things will happen: the strongest economic units, trust and monopolies, will secure the available labour power by the simple means of offering the highest price for it, and those who find in the provision of luxury goods the most profitable market will absorb many of the raw materials. A motor firm engaged in the curious form of publicity known as "prestige advertising" recently painted a picture of the "new world for which we are fighting" as one in which the roads would be "gay with cars". It is not a form of "gaiety" which appeals to all of us, perhaps, but it appeals to a sufficient number to have created a danger that we might have realized the picture at the cost of leaving other roads grey with slums.

Estimates as to how long this phase of spontaneous full employment will last must be largely speculative. We do not know enough about the economic conditions consequent on the defeat of Germany to make any prophecy worth while. The period during which "the job will look for the man " (as ideally it always ought to do), and not the man for the job, may last longer than many dare to hope that it will, but with a return, however gradual, to the normal operation of a world-wide industrialism, nothing like full employment will automatically persist. It is not for Christian sociologists to wring their hands over such a prospect; it is rather for them to face in good time and realistically the challenges with which a developed technology faces Western man in respect of his work. I will only mention three, and can say no more about these than is necessary to indicate what their nature is.

1. The first is the need for detaching the means of subsistence from its identification—in principle, at any rate—with the reward for labour, and recognizing that as man exists in a dual capacity, as a citizen and as a worker, his means of livelihood should come to him in two forms. Our society has been forced to go some way in this direction already by its payment of social pensions and grants of all kinds and its impending acceptance of the principle of Family Allowances. But it has not clearly faced the logic of the fact that a large proportion of the wealth of a modern generation comes to it as a heritage from the energies and ingenuities of men of an earlier day, which logic suggests that a proportion of the income of its citizens should accrue to them as an unconditional share in this heritage, or what some have called a social dividend. Exploration of the subject would lead to that region of sociological jungle known as monetary reform, into which you would no doubt be only less reluctant to follow me than I should be to lead. But I am confident that while we cling to the idea that there is no valid or feasible way of making a sufficient livelihood for men than by making work for them, whether that work is necessary or not, we shall never arrive at a true judgment of what work is and what it ought to be.

2. A too-little-realized danger of the acceptance of the permanent validity of "full employment" as a social goal is its effect in the multiplication of meretricious products. For if the vast capacity of modern power production is to be maintained at full strength in order to maximize employment, then the consumer may have to be forcibly fed with an endless output of largely superfluous gadgets in order to absorb its output, and "conditioned" into a never-ending acceptance of new and spurious "needs" (disguised no doubt as "a higher

standard of living") by that most parasitic of all occupations, high-power salesmanship. For it is a peril of mass-production that it has a tendency to enforce mass-consumption. Christians, concerned at once with the quality of man's life and the validity of his work, have the duty to insist that while employment on mass-production *ought* to diminish, employment on qualitative production is not subject to the same limits of usefulness. Since this latter type of production is one for which our countrymen have a traditional aptitude, and one which will often constitute the sole justification for (and perhaps possibility of) our entering or remaining in world markets—so far as this may be necessary for obtaining imports which we genuinely require, too much attention can hardly be given to this aspect of our economy.

3. While a good deal of nonsense has been talked (on one side or another) about the "Leisure State", it is undeniable that industrialism has forced far too many of our people to work at routine processes, in offices as well as in factories, for far too large a proportion of their lives. Such workers need not only—indeed, perhaps not so much—longer holidays, as more alternation of occupation between organized industry and self-sought activity in garden, allotment and private workshop. One of the worst consequences of nearly two centuries of industrialism is the undermining of the capacity of the ordinary man to organize his own life. It is for Christians to see that the exaltation of "Full Employment" does not blind society to the need to strive for a state of things in which power production is not endlessly extended, but used more and more to release men for the exercise of discrimination and self-control in the handling of "free time".

Connected with the problem of Employment is that "full mobility of labour" explicitly endorsed in the Government's White Paper. The phrase has such a technical ring that it may not be immediately obvious that it has any implications

for the Christian Sociologist at all. Nevertheless, since the
manner of its implementation would affect the personal,
domestic, civic and ecclesiastical life of the ordinary man and
woman in certain very radical ways, we ought to be aware of
what may easily be concealed in it. Industrialism has always
tended to regard its "labour power" as a mobile force which
ought to move at the beck and call of the "labour market";
labour exchanges, one of the most characteristic of twentieth-
century "reforms", were designed to facilitate this. Such
mobility is not, of course, inherently vicious in all circumstances. A certain amount of change of scene and experience
is generally welcomed by young workers and of value to them,
nor can any developed economy be expected to standardize
its production for ever in the areas where it originates. A
certain amount of "fluidity" is natural, and the difficulties it
may occasion are not beyond the power of social organization
to meet without unreasonable sacrifices being demanded of
the human agents of production.

   But there are grave dangers implicit in a situation in which
the idea of "mobility of labour" is established as a normal
method of implementing a centralized control of production.
"In an expanding economy," says the White Paper, "workers
must be ready and able to move freely between one occupation and another." This is, of course, one of the two things
they have been required to do during war-time—the other
being to "stay put" on "essential work", and the control of
labour which these requirements afford is one of the two conditions (the other being the "unlimited market") which has
enabled the Government to maintain the "full employment" which the war emergency necessitates. These powers
of "direction", which have been extremely unpopular with the
workers over whom they have been exercised, are just the sort
of regulations that a Government which takes employment
as its primary goal must have been tempted to prolong. The

temptation must have been strengthened by the existence of a large number of camps and barracks which could be conveniently turned over to certain sorts of mass production, with the "mobilized" workers housed on the spot.

Is there anything in all this of which we ought to be apprehensive from the standpoint of a Christian view of man? I think that there is, and on four grounds which I can only summarize briefly. First, because such discretion in the hands of public authorities involves at least the possibility of grave infringements of human liberty and is a move towards a servile State. Secondly, for its obvious dangers to the solidarity of family life, already seriously threatened by all the multitudinous dispersions enforced by war. Thirdly, from the standpoint of religion, since "mobility" imperils that attachment to an Altar and to the habits of a regular spiritual life which is so important for the development of that *"Koinonia"* which is gravely lacking in so many of our congregations. And fourthly, for a reason less obvious, but not perhaps less important than these. Our society suffers already, though more perhaps among the middle class than in other sections of the community, from a "nomadic" tendency, as a consequence of which men take no root in the places in which they fugitively reside. Nothing is more urgent now than an effort so to replan our community life as to re-establish conditions in which not only can houses become true homes, but those who dwell in them can develop a sense of civic responsibility for the place in which they live. This will be difficult enough to do in any case, but if we were to go through a period—or, still worse, establish a habit—of government "direction" to the breadwinner by which he could be moved round from one place to another as might be most convenient to those who were organizing "reconstruction" on a national scale, the task would become insuperable, and a lasting injury be inflicted to the domestic and civic life of our people.

G

It is for Christian opinion to set the needs and the rights of the worker, his family and his locality against the pleas of administrative "efficiency". One way to do this is to demand that as a general principle work shall be brought to the worker rather than the worker to the work. No doubt there are plenty of cases in which, for sufficient reasons, this principle cannot be applied, but it will make all the difference if we have this criterion by which to test public policy in general, and specific exemplifications of it. Beyond this, however, there are certain tendencies which can be encouraged so as to render a legitimate fluidity of labour harmless, and even salutary. One is the increase of those enterprises, somewhat misleadingly known as "trading estates", which are explicitly designed to turn over from one type of production to another as changes in demand suggest. Again, it would be highly desirable that the training schemes in the post-war situation, first adumbrated in the White Paper, should be devised to teach the worker a variety of skills, rendering possible an alternation of occupation. The effect of both these developments would be to increase the "fluidity" of the labourer without requiring him to break up his home at the direction of a Government department, or in obedience to a fatalistically accepted economic trend.

Both "Full Employment" and "Mobility of Labour" represent the way in which a post-Christian society, uninformed by any doctrine of man or philosophy of work, tends to react to the sort of economic pressures which so easily appear to be irresistible. It does so by seeking to manipulate man rather than by resolving to dominate and control social factors in his interest. But if Christians are effectively to counter the fallacies and perils implicit in these slogans it will not be by a blind denunciation of them, but by constructive efforts to show that what is legitimate in the policies they embody can be achieved by means which involve neither a maiming of

man nor a distortion of the productive process from a misunderstanding of both. This will call for much more independence of thought from Christians than they have been
accustomed to display hitherto, and for a determined effort
not to be enslaved to ideologies and sectarian habits of mind
which have no roots in the soil of Christian civilization. If we
are resolved to demand that work shall be accepted as valid in
proportion as it is at once a ministry, a vocation and a partnership, we shall have a standard by which to test not only the
programmes of a secular reconstruction, but those mental
attitudes by which the characteristics of a culture are formed
and maintained. The social diseases of our time are less the
result of evil will than of false ideas; Christians are therefore
summoned to contribute not only to a moral but even more to
an intellectual reconstruction. This must be both a short-
term and a long-term process. In a desire to avoid giving a
too academic complexion to this paper, I have dealt at some
length with problems of the immediate post-war situation. I
have therefore left myself little space in which to deal with
two other matters of capital importance, though of a more
"long-term" character. Yet I cannot close without a reference, however brief, to two of the main challenges which
contemporary industry presents to our culture. We may
designate them as the problem of technique and the problem
of control.

From the standpoint of Christian sociology these two problems are aspects of a single issue: how to make industrial
achievement subordinate to the doctrine of vocation. This
doctrine is the Christian counter to the fatalism of a secularized economics, which always tends towards making man a
tool of an industrial process that is the product of his intelligence but so easily becomes a vehicle of his pride and will to
domination. This is especially true of societies like our own,
in which the ingenuities of human contrivance divert atten-

tion from—and even banish the spectacle of—God's work in
nature. For the dweller in Leeds or Birmingham an "un-
balanced economy" is not merely a social error: it is a
psychological disaster, for it unbalances not only his nation's
economic activities but his own judgment, since all that he
sees around him appears only as the work of man. So far the
spectacle of industrialism has been so unattractive aesthetically
that man's pride in it has been in some measure restrained;
it required more assurance than even a Victorian capitalist
could easily muster up to believe that man had made a better
job of the Black Country than God had made of the green
fields that lay beyond it. But with the deposition of steam
by electricity, and the elaboration of a "functional", stream-
lined architecture in which to house both the dynamos and
the calculating machines, and even it may be those who "feed"
them, this check may be removed. The townsman will see
nature no longer as a co-operator, nor even in the aesthetic
sphere as a successful competitor: "harnessed" to his power
production, nature will appear only as a slave.

There is but one way for man to recover his initiative
against the works of his hands, and that is to find the right
place for them and keep them in it. And the place of tools in
the hierarchy of human activity is not first but fourth. Man
exists for God; natural resources exist that man may co-
operate with them to continue, as a "partaker in the divine
nature", some activity which God as Creator has begun;
his intelligence exists (among other more exalted purposes)
to help him to devise the best means of doing so. These
means, which began as manual tools, have culminated in the
vast power-driven engines of to-day, but they are still tools,
and if man does not use his tools in accordance with their
true nature—and his—they will soon begin to use him. For
the sphere of the machine cannot be "neutralized"; if it is
not directed to good ends it will work for evil ones. And we

have no right to blame the technician for that; ends are not his business, and, as Mr. T. M. Heron has said, "only the technician who is also a saint can withstand a constant succession of offers to use his talents in the wrong direction".[1]

The true problem of machinery, then, is how man is to learn to use it instead of being used by it. We have hardly begun to think about this yet, much less to do anything about it. Modern technics have developed under the secularist (sometimes miscalled "humanist") influences which have dominated "Renaissance Man", for whom the achievement of power has been ever a primary consideration. It has been assumed, almost without discussion, that all that man can do —or force those dependent on him to do—he must be free to do. The very idea of Vocation is inverted: it is the call of the Machine that man must answer, not the call of God. Behind this idolatry of technics are two of modern man's most characteristic vices: his pride and his insatiableness. The technological problem is thus at bottom a religious one: its solution involves the cure of sin and the acknowledgment of divine purpose. We cannot use the enormous capacities of modern industrialism aright until we know what we should use them *for*. So far we have used them without discrimination and without restraint, and then tried to alleviate their more obviously destructive effects by "social reforms". But this is to approach the problem from the wrong end. Let our motto rather be, "Take care of man and the wheels will take care of themselves".

We still speak of an occupation as a "calling", which is, of course, precisely what the word "vocation" means. But man can only feel "called" to do a job which, as we say, "appeals" to him. This does not, of course, mean that he will enjoy himself all the time that he is engaged on it, that he will never

[1] Article on "The Function of Industry" in *Christendom*, June 1942, p. 95.

get tired of it, and never feel that he would rather be doing something else. "Joy in work", like most other kinds of human happiness, is not something which can be guaranteed in advance in whatever circumstances it is sought, and indeed the more consciously it *is* sought, the less likely it is to be experienced. When it comes it is as a by-product of a task at once worth doing and well done; real and rewarding, yet fugitive and evanescent. And rightly so, for since work is not an absolute end, men ought not to look for total satisfaction in it; to do so would be idolatry, the idolatry so well exhibited in "the irritating optimism of working-class religions".[1] Man is not intended to find his own meaning in his work, but he must find *a* meaning in it, and there is nothing more hostile to the Christian conception of vocation than the sheer meaninglessness of so much that our irrational economic system, sets its "hands" to do, dominated as it is by the "employment hypothesis" and the need to create markets for the gadgets it multiplies so aimlessly. It is only if a thing is really worth doing that it is worth doing well, and the first condition of a vocation is that the activity for which it calls should be worthy of the man who is to exercise it. The second is that he should be worthy of it, which he will not be if his talents do not lie in this direction. And, as we have noted already, in a healthy society the job would look for the man and not vice versa. To quote Mr. Heron again: "There is no scientific method of organization which ensures that the man shall always be set to the right job, but there is plenty of evidence to show that the right job always calls to the right man". It is for society to see that men are in a position to hear such calls and free to respond to them.

Vocation is essentially a personal thing. But it is not therefore one which isolates a person from his fellows. For one man called to a solitary vocation a hundred are called into an

[1] Borne and Henry, op. cit., p. 141.

association of activity with their fellows, yet it is all too seldom—and in industry almost never—that they are in truth associated vocationally. It is the burden of Dr. Peter Drucker's book that "the future of industrial man" depends on our power to reconstitute society so as to give the worker of every kind a status in it appropriate to contemporary realities. Our industry is still organized on the assumption that the control of it ought to—and can—be exercised by stockholders according to the amount of their financial interests. But, as Drucker points out, not only is it impossible for those whose interest in the matter is purely acquisitive to exercise industrial control, but this is the last thing the bulk of them wish to do. "The stockholder has abdicated . . . to him his rights are nothing but burdens; they are entirely contrary to his purpose in becoming a stockholder."[1]

Some have looked for an end to this anomalous situation in a "managerial revolution" by which authority in industry would pass over, in fact and in form, from financially interested directors and stockholders to an alliance of works managers and technical specialists. Whether or not this is what is likely to happen—and there are social elements with their roots in money-power which will be much concerned to see that it does not happen—it is certainly not what Christian teaching would lead us to think ought to happen. "Functional" control may be better than financial control, but if it is to be exercised by an oligarchy interested primarily in technical possibilities of mass-production and maximum output, the cause of man will not be greatly advanced. I have contended that Christian doctrine demands that work should be not only a ministry and a vocation but the basis of a partnership by which the wage system characteristic of a secularized industrialism is transcended. To achieve such a

[1] *The Future of Industrial Man*, p. 56.

transformation was the object of the first "Christian Socialists" a century ago; sixty years later a similar purpose inspired
one of the most vital and significant movements which this
country has produced. The Guild Socialists may have conceived their aims in too sectarian a spirit and based their
policies upon an unrealistic estimate of the power of initiative
and constructive organization latent in the trade unions to
which they primarily appealed. But they did point to the
need for two things without which an organization of industry satisfactory alike to Christian social tradition and the
psychological needs of the worker will not be achieved. One
is the "constitutionalizing" of industries as public bodies with
a defined professional status, which we might well call Guilds,
on which representatives of every grade and type of those co-
operating in the industry would combine to envisage and
define its purposes and assume a share in its responsible control. The other is opportunity for a voice in the day-to-day
decisions of the work-shop for all those whom they affect.
Christians have a direct interest in seeing that efforts are made
to move forward in both these directions,[1] for until they are,
whatever other improvements our economic system may
manifest, the vast majority of its human agents will remain
without the status appropriate to man as Christian doctrine
defines him. And a society which does not understand what
man is will never discover what work ought to be.

[1] A challenging book which throws much light on this subject is *Lost
Property* by Paul Derrick (Dennis Dobson; 1947).

VI. OUR CULTURE: ITS RELIGION

by

V. A. Demant

The lectures which precede this concluding one have shown that the crisis of our modern culture is in some deep way bound up with a crisis in its religion. This has now to be examined by itself.

It is often said by ecclesiastical apologists that our Western European culture has been formed by Christianity. That is but half a truth. Much of what we call the civilization of Europe derives from two other sources—from the thought and institutions of the ancient world and also from the particular racial and social dispositions of the various European peoples. It is impossible to say, however, how these forces would have developed if the outlooks of classical antiquity had not been given a new character and, indeed, had not been revived and carried into history by the Christian Church, or if the characteristics of European populations had been untouched by Christian life and thought. We may say that these two influences represent given facts, and that in dealing with them the Christian religion gave a specific character to European society and was at the same time clothed in the variegated garments woven by them.

An opposite view had been maintained from time to time—namely, that Christianity has tended to disintegrate the natural civilization of European man. The historian Gibbon represented this view, and Nietzsche regarded Christianity as the vampire of civilization, which, for him, meant the influence of Greece and Rome. Julian the Apostate was their forerunner in the fourth century. There are critics to-day who hold that what is positively in the human interest in the modern world has been achieved by constant struggle against the alleged reactionary influence of the Church, and particularly against its other-worldliness. Let us see what there is in these two views, and ask how far the traditional culture of Europe is a Christian product and to what extent Christianity is a danger to civilization, and try to relate these questions to the crisis of our time.

Before we go farther into these questions there is a preliminary consideration to be borne in mind in judging the dispositions of a culture and what happens to it, just as it is necessary in estimating the character of a man. It is that neither the dispositions of a culture nor the character of a man can be judged by making an arithmetic comparison of the good and bad points, or the strong and weak elements in either case. There are creative and destructive elements in every culture, and the net result is not to be assessed by making, however accurately, a list of each and seeing which list is longer than the other. What counts is the way they are mixed. One man may have ten good points and six bad ones; another have five good points and twelve bad ones. But the second man may be by far the finer person if one of his few good points is, say, the virtue of gratitude, humour or humility. Number one may lack this entirely, and for want of this ingredient his other good points will be impaired in their effect on his total character. In the same way, the culture of a period or a people may have a number of creative and healthy elements and still be in a state of decline, if there are one or two destructive forces in it that have the power to infect the whole. In addition, an influence composed of several elements can have a formative and creative effect on a period, but if one of these loses its force, then the other remaining elements may become not only ineffective, but also by themselves become positively disruptive. In my opening lecture I suggested that something like this happened to our modern culture. The aims or values of Christendom have been to a large extent retained, but the assumptions about the nature of existence have been replaced by others. Shall we say, using technical terms, that our cultural crisis is due to the *ethos* derived from Christianity having become separated from and deprived of its specific *logos*. In other words, certain dispositions in respect of action, will, behaviour, have been formed by Christian dogma and cultus; these dispositions remain operative after the word, the doctrine, the shape of things, out of which the dispositions were born have disappeared. What man does to the universe remains as a habit: what the universe says to him is now something entirely different. And it is possible that, as I hinted, an *ethos* without its proper *logos* may be not merely lacking in support, but may be, by that very lack, destructive in its effects. We can put it another way. Religion has two movements: piety and spirituality. Piety is reverence for the gods, for the universe, for the greater than man; spirituality is the activity of the spirit-centred creature, and can be exercised either under a sense of piety or in emancipation from it. It describes not only the religious acts of response to God and His creation, but also every activity directed towards society and the physical world in which man exerts his spiritual superiority to his natural environment. In this sense thought, industry, politics are spiritual activities. They are possible only to a creature who has a certain inner freedom from the cycle of the earth's life. Therefore we could also describe the predicament of the modern world as arising out of *spirituality* without *piety*.

How has this come about? It is impossible, I think, to exaggerate the extent to which Christianity has stimulated the sense of individuality in European man. This does not normally arrest our attention, because we are the heirs of that influence, and we accept it as if it were a natural part of the human heritage. Only after long and deep acquaintance with the history of human cultures does it become striking what an extraordinary being Western man has been and still is. He has shown an energy, restlessness and enterprise, a cerebration and will, in comparison with which all other societies, however civilized, look relatively vegetative. The self, the individual standing over against the rest of reality—that is the outstanding characteristic of the European and his cultural progeny in other parts of the world.[1] And the gradual isolation of this "over-against" outlook from any counterbalancing attitude of being involved, of respect, of discipleship, is no small part of the crisis of the modern world.

Now, Christianity had a great deal to do with sealing this sense of individuality in the soul of man, though the beginnings of the tendency go back to Greek thought, and even perhaps farther, to the craft of the magician seeking to bend things to human desire. The late Sir Edwyn Bevan describes the impulse given to this vast turn in human consciousness by the Greek world:

> "It was because the Greeks could stand off from established custom and ask the reason why, that they could make political progress. . . . All the development of knowledge, of command over the forces of nature, of purposeful order, which is

[1] Waldo Frank, explaining the success of the Spaniards in Peru, writes: "The Spaniard believed in his own person. The most real reality of his world was his individual soul and his individual body, which though it must die, would rise again in the last days. . . . All experience is referred to the will, all his life ruled by it, all time is made for it. . . . To meet the Spaniard there were no *persons* in Peru. There was only the Ayllu. And the will of the Ayllu though persistent was not aggressive. . . . It was a will delimited by the apparent surface of nature. The Indian could not grasp, could not believe what he beheld. The notion of mortal man sailing across a trackless sea dismayed him. Still more inconceivable was the lust and will of these men. Their every deed of daring, bestiality and devotion (indissolubly mixed in the conquistador) had a dimension which the Indian mind could not reach."—*America Hispana*, pp. 54–57. Quoted in Reinhold Niebuhr, *Moral Man and Immoral Society*, p. 43.

meant by the term Western civilization to-day, has had for
its moving principle a rationalism whose origin is to be found
in the Greek City-states."[1]

This attitude, which stands off from the whole moving flux
of concrete existence and asks the reason why, begins a process in which the individuality of man is set over against the
rest of reality. This is both the triumph and perhaps the
doom of European man.

Now, the Christian religion strengthened this tendency to
set the individuality of man over against the mere stream
of life, and also kept it in check by its dogmas and rituals.
Christianity served to emancipate the human being in the
depths of his soul, not merely in his mind as the Greeks had
done, from being merely a part of the tribal or social or the
natural process.[2] But at the same time it bore in upon him
his utterly dependent participation in a "cosmic" whole
through the unique relation between God and man which the
Church inculcated. I want to deal briefly with a few ways in
which Christianity has served to form the outlook of Western
man, and to lead up to the conclusion that we are faced with
a situation in the twentieth century which compels us to look
upon it as the end of a span as long as Christian history itself,
if not longer still.

First of all, what sense of his place and significance did
man get from Christianity? To answer this we have to see
how human existence is felt and thought of in the relation of
the eternal and the temporal worlds. All great religions are
concerned with the distinctions and connections of these two
realities: the world of nature and history, of time and change
on the one side, and an eternal world above and behind the

[1] Edwyn Bevan, *Christianity and Hellenism*, pp. 14–15.
[2] This has often been appreciated by the critics of the Christian religion
who have condemned it for this very reason, men like Comte, Feuerbach
and Karl Marx, and to a lesser degree Robert Owen.

flux of things on the other. Broadly speaking there are three accounts of their relation. One holds that only the eternal timeless world is real. The world of events is illusory, or a snare, or a bad joke, or a nuisance, or a fallen and depraved condition. Salvation for man in this case consists in freeing himself from its falsifying and limiting conditions. In the main this is the outlook of Oriental religious philosophies and some dominant aspects of Greek thought. The temporal order is explained away as a deformation of the eternal.

Another type is the opposite of this. It regards the temporal process only as real. This underlies the teaching of ancients like Heraclitus and the Stoics, and of moderns like Hegel and Karl Marx. We may say that it is the working assumption of the modern world. I want to emphasize, however, that the character of this world-view is not necessarily materialistic or naturalistic, though these are its most rigorous forms of expression. It may have a religious and spiritual dress. The point is that for this view the source of meaning in the world process is to be found somewhere within that process. Its deity is entirely an immanent principle.

The Jewish and Christian outlook regards both the eternal and the temporal worlds as real and significant, and have a peculiar version of the relation between them. While Jehovah is the "high and lofty one that inhabiteth eternity", He is also the Lord of History for whom a thousand years are as one day and one day as a thousand years.

History is a process of real events, an irreversible pattern of happenings that do matter—and they matter not only because of their roots in the past or for their effects in the future, they matter supremely because each event has a significance in the sight of the Transcendent God and makes a mark upon the eternal slate. The way in which this outlook has given the Western world its intense interest in history has now a large literature.[1] It should be noted that man makes history only when he sees himself as to some extent standing above it—when he has as it were a transcendent vantage point from which to relate the present to the past and future. A being entirely immersed in the process would be unaware of, and uninterested in, the meaning of the process.

The doctrine of Creation is important in this respect. It means that the world and its career have a meaning, a purpose; but also that the key to its meaning does not lie in the world itself, but its relation to God who is above and independent of it. In addition, living and spiritual parts of the universe, like man himself, his histories, communities and actions, are significant in themselves in relation to the Divine will and purpose, and not only because they participate in the whole world-process. This is what Kierkegaard meant when he said, "The individual finds his relation to the universal through his relation to the absolute, and not his relation to the absolute through his relation to the universal".

Christianity stretched this insight still farther. It made the relation of each man to the eternal God a precise relation to the person of Jesus the Christ, in whose flesh the eternal irrupts into time. He is the second Adam, the republication of the origin of all things; He appears, dies and rises from death at the "end of the times"—anticipating the end when history will be wound up and its meaning fully disclosed.

He speaks to each man of every time in terms of love, grace, hope and judgment, and thereby places him in a realm of existence which cuts completely across the groupings in which he participates as a part of the world-process, such groupings as his tribe, city, empire associations and their histories. All this tended to give Western man a consciousness that history

---

[1] See e.g., *The Kingdom of God and History*, Church, Community and State Series, by various writers (Allen and Unwin). N. Berdyaev, *The Meaning of History* (G. Bles). Christopher Dawson, *Progress and Religion* (Sheed and Ward). P. Tillich, *The Interpretation of History* (Scribner).

was not a mere flux; it could be discerned as a cosmic-spiritual drama. But it was a drama enacted in terms of two worlds: the temporal or *this* age, and the eternal world or the powers of the age to come.

There was thus developed a sense of the significance of events—each standing as it were at the intersection of two worlds—and also of human responsibility and individuality, and following from these tendencies a sense of the significance of history, of man's responsibility for events. In consequence of these there grew a disposition for the human being to see himself as over against the natural given substance of his world. I mean the substance out of which he comes and which is the foundation of all his actions, especially the biological, tribal and social substance of all human existence. Later, when the modern period had heightened this disposition and at the same time rejected the cosmic-spiritual scheme and the divine-human context out of which the dispositions had grown, then great dangers were ahead. Something Christianity had made possible now acquired an independent existence. The discovery of man's inner world due to the link between the centre of his being and the Supreme Spirit—in fact, the discovery of the soul, which could be contrasted with the universe—when this was emancipated from its religious context it produced the whole ethos of the modern world. This meant that man's inner being and the universe on which it looked stood nakedly confronting one another without deep awareness that both inner and outer world had a common source, unity and dependence in the living God.

I cannot in this lecture go into all the consequences of this transformation, the change by which man's relative superiority to the universe was changed into an independence and an "over-against" attitude. Pascal gave expression to the truth and to the deformation of the truth. Everybody knows that he said, "By space the universe encompasses me as a pin point; by thought I encompass it"—but few have taken notice of what follows when he says, "Reality cannot be measured by our concepts (that is by the general ideas the mind forms by leaving out all that is individual and unique) or by what we designate the 'possible', but what is possible as well as our concepts must be measured by reality".

Nowhere has the tendency of rationalist accounts of man's world and idealistic thought been more harmful than in the social and economic sphere. Take just one instance which has had far-reaching effects. Our modern industrial society got into its stride under the influence of an abstract theory of human needs and behaviour—namely, that men would always act from motives of the maximum economic gain, buying cheapest and selling dearest, irrespective of boundaries of family, class and nation. In other words, the real world of men and women, with their attachments, loyalties, hopes and fears, moral and religious convictions, was supposed to be amenable to purely economic incentives in a free market. It was assumed that all other motives would give place to the maximum of buying and selling of land, labour, commodities and even money. This is what I mean by a rationalistic explanation of human life, for it is a picture made by the rational intellect in abstraction from the reality of human existence. Actually this economic "paradise" hardly got going before society in all sorts of ways started protecting itself against its tendency to dissolve all the realities of social living. All forms of socialism, whether democratic, communist or fascist, are vast measures of "protection" against the gale set blowing by the attempt to put purely economic rationality into practice. In seeking so to protect the realities of labour, family, neighbourhood, race-groups and nations from dissolution, men in the twentieth century are, of course, openly or undesignedly making for the undoing of the whole

H

European and Christian attachment to the significance of the person. It is a judgment upon the perversion of man's discovery of himself, which has led him to try to impose his inner creations upon the real world. I have referred to this social and economic issue as an example—the case could be extended to the realms of thought and literature and politics. In many ways the twentieth century represents a revolt against the "liberalism" of the modern period which sought to emancipate man from his roots in God and in the material world. Therefore I think this period of judgment can only be transcended by a double reverse process. There will have to be a real return to the discipline of the inner life in religion. The current offering of the Christian moral pill for the ills of the world won't do. At the same time we need a recovery of the older scientific spirit which had some respect for the universe, and this includes the whole context of human living. This must replace the current pseudo-scientific know-all mania for adjusting, conditioning and adapting man to anything the technical experts can do with the physical material.

The serious point I am trying to illustrate is that we are living in a post-Christian world. That does not mean an age which has merely succeeded in time the centuries when Christian Faith and doctrine formed men's minds and has dropped that faith and doctrine. "Post-Christian" is, as I use the term, the description of our age, whose problems would not be nearly as acute, nor would they show the character they have, but for the dispositions I have referred to—the dispositions in regard to man's relation to the world formed by and now separated from the specific Christian world-view. This shows that Christianity is a highly dangerous religion, for the world would not have had these cataclysmic tensions and problems if it had remained pagan and if paganism had recovered its vitality.

What we have to do with to-day is a twofold influence:

first the hang-over from the modern humanist period. This includes that faith in the inner world of man and power over things, without God, in relation to whom that inner world came alive. It includes the tremendous sense of responsibility for events and faith in action, without obedience to the laws of being—those laws which have to be rediscovered again and again by contemplation and reverent discipleship towards the real world of man's total existence. It includes a faith in the significance of history, without the theology of the Kingdom of God which is both the fulfilment and the judgment upon history; so we still live under the illusion of "Progress" which equates the direction the most furious activity is taking with an inevitable march to "the one far-off divine event to which the whole creation moves". The other half of our contemporary situation is the revolt against all this humanism and progressivism in the name of political and social solidarity and expediency. That is what I mean by the twentieth century reversing the whole meaning of the Christian revolution; but I must point out again that it is society's own inevitable protection against the disintegrating effects of modern man's fantasy of himself as master of reality.

Now let us look at this story from another point of view. The double relation of man to the eternal and temporal orders has given a certain character to European culture. It has done so by introducing a "duality" into the very substance of society, a duality between the historic communities in which men found themselves and the society of the Church, with its supernatural and trans-local character. A Christian who belonged, say, to Corinth or Rome in the fourth century, or to Paris or Norwich of the fourteenth, had to maintain an allegiance both to his local community and government and to a Church which over-arched all other divisions made by nature and history. That is to say, his obligations to his temporal community were not supreme and all-embracing. Over and over again considerations of expediency and social solidarity had to give place to demands of a different order. There was henceforth always a problem of distinguishing between the things that belong to God and those that belong to Caesar.

Now, this tension of two loyalties, which is the essence of Christian history, does not exist where loyalty to God is part of loyalty to the earthly community—that is, where the earthly community is the mediator of the word of divinity to man—it exists only when there is a word which man can hear and answer, spoken in and through another independent voice. Nor does this specifically Christian tension exist when the temporal order is confronted only with an invisible, purely inward Church. It exists only when the temporal community and its organizations are confronted on the same historic plane with an institution of the Church which cuts across them, forming a different network of loyalties. The story of this tension is a long and interesting one; it has often been shown to be the condition of that growth of liberty which has so specially marked the culture of the West. Where the ruling power of government, custom or folk-soul could always be called to account by the subject in the name of the wider and deeper allegiance to a universal Church, there the submergence of the person in the social whole was largely held in check. And the effectiveness of this check does not depend on the spiritual power being always pure and disinterested in its religious service, as it most certainly was not always; it depends merely on its being a counter authority.

Now, it seems to me that something has happened in this matter of double loyalties similar to what I tried to describe in the matter of the Christian world-view. We in the twentieth century are in danger of trying to overcome the disintegration of the last three centuries by returning to a pre-Christian situation. I have hit upon an analogy to illustrate what I mean, which of course must not be pressed too rigidly. The analogy is drawn from the relation of the sexes. Just as there is a form of life in which there is no differentiation between female and male, no polarity, so there is a large part of human history covering both tribal and civilized cultures, where there is no differentiation, no polarity, between society and religion. That is the case in the ancient empires and also, in a less absolute form, in the Hebrew Church-State. Christianity, inaugurated by Christ with a Church that was supernatural and trans-local, brought about immediately, by its very nature, a duality between society and Church analogous to that of female and male in the bi-sexual situation of living things. This duality was not by any means a dualism, though at certain points there were open and deep clashes. Shall we say playfully, but seriously, that the first three centuries of the Christian era correspond to the stage at which there is meeting between young woman and young man. The period from the conversion of Constantine to the end of the eighth century is like the period of engagement. The epoch from that date, with the coronation of Charlemagne, to the fifteenth century is represented in our analogy by marriage, with its tensions and mutual interaction. The sixteenth century witnesses a divorce. Here our analogy gets a bit confused, for while the workaday world finds more purely secular modes of guidance and religion becomes more merely inward and moralizing after the secular event instead of directing it, there is also a move such as we had in England under Henry VIII with parallels elsewhere, to make the Church an accommodating agent of the national enterprise. But on the whole the essential duality of Church and society steadily ceased to operate because of a separation between them.[1]

[1] For a fuller treatment of this point I might refer to my article "Religion and the State" in *Recall to Religion* (Eyre and Spottiswoode), reprinted in a forthcoming collection of essays, *Theology of Society* (Faber).

Now, in the twentieth century there have been many signs that society needs a religious foundation for its culture. As the sociological and cultural pattern of European society was breaking up, and as the greater Churches had given up the task of social and cultural formation, it was natural that society itself should produce its own religion on its own immanentist assumptions. It had to overcome the agnosticism and piecemeal scepticism of the late humanist period. So we have in various forms a deification of society itself, each with its own myth. Communism with its class messianism, Fascism with its cult of the national heritage, and National Socialism with its race mysticism, are all examples of a swing towards a society which is its own Church. Comte and Fuerbach in the nineteenth century had hoped that "Humanity" would be the divinity of the future. History has shown that "Humanity" is too general and abstract a conception, and it is certain limited and definite movements of human existence in history that have taken on the absolute character of revealed truth and "priestly" supremacy. In other words, in order to overcome the disintegrating effects of the post-sixteenth-century divorce of religion and society, the modern world is reverting to the pre-Christian "hermaphrodite" relation, in which Church and society are one thing. The whole span of Christian history has come round full circle, and we had better face it squarely.

To face it squarely means to recognize that this turn of affairs is not due initially to totalitarian and dictorial policies, for we are witnessing something deeper than the old problem of Church and State. It is rather that omnipotent and absolute governments arise from and respond to the same social forces by which society seeks to protect itself from disintegrating by a purely "societal" religion.[1] Mr. Christopher Dawson describes the situation:

[1] I apologize for this ugly word "societal". But neither "national" nor "ethnic" quite covers all its manifestations.

"Human nature needs a holy community, and though this
need finds satisfaction in a true Christian Order, it does not
find it in the sect or the chapel which was all the nineteenth
century offered to fill the void left by the secular State.
Hence granted the scandal of Christian disunion and the
failure of the Church to inspire and mould the subordinate
categories of social life, it was inevitable that men should seek
satisfaction elsewhere, in a community that was wider than
that of the sect and deeper and richer than that of the secular
state."[1]

The very same urge to have a religion which is identical
with society's own feeling and aspirations and need of
solidarity is operating in the "democratic" communities.
Here the social drift has not taken an open political form, and
it clothes itself very largely in the terminology of the Christian
Faith. In Britain and the United States especially is it almost
true that, as Santayana said with but slight exaggeration, "All
modern religion is but social reform, whatever its nominal
creed". Such a "societal" religion, which uses the idiom of
traditional Christianity while propounding, often unconscious
of the issue, an outlook which has completely dissolved the
tension between God's operation in grace and the Church
and His operation in nature and society, may be a more serious
menace to the Faith and to men in society than definite
unbelief. It represents an undogmatic, unsupernatural and
unevangelical religion. It equates Christianity with good
ideals, grace with moral and social aims and the Holy Ghost
with the spirit of man at its highest. It attaches no real vital
meaning to sin, sanctification and redemption. It has lost
the sense of the distinction between, and complimentary
character of revealed religion and natural religion, and it
has lost the polarity of these two which made up the real
influence of Christianity upon our civilization.

I am afraid a great deal of what is wanted (out of pure
intention) in the way of reunion of the Churches, of religious

[1] *Beyond Politics* (Sheed and Ward), pp. 131 ff.

education without denominational differences and of the
application of Christianity to our social life, is on this plane
of society's own naturally evolved religion, which still utters
the terminology of the New Testament and Church theology.
In fact, I think we are approaching something on the scale of
the Arian controversy in the early days of the Church. In the
Arian heresy there was the attempt to express a Greek
theology, with its two levels in the Godhead, in the idiom of
the Christian Faith.

Now we have attempts to express an immanentist, dyna-
mistic, pelagian religion also in the idiom of Christianity.
You will also have noticed how the calendar of the Church's
year is being invaded and displaced by society's own commemoration of events and good causes; and how the specific
language of the Church services is adapted to reflect the
topical sentiments and needs of the period. In very many
ways the presuppositions of the Christian world view are
being given up, though its language is used to clothe the
rival presuppositions of the day, and in many cases those
who most confidently carry this on in the hope that they are
expressing Christianity in contemporary idiom are in fact
expressing the assumptions of the day before yesterday in the
hallowed words of the Christian tradition.

While this tendency of our time must be seen as a threat
to overturn the whole span of Christian history, our attitude
to it should be understandingly sympathetic as well as
critical.

The move towards an unsupernatural, uneschatological
religion is the outcome of a real need of the modern soul.
The world-order has lost its bearings through the schism
between the natural and social basis of human life and the
transcendent God, which schism has marked the whole
modern period since the sixteenth century. Modern man is
torn between the opposite pulls of his social situation and his

moral aims. Christians seem to have been blind to the deep crisis of the modern world, and have thought they could cure a serious spiritual wound by moral advice. Our rational, liberal, democratic society therefore evolves its own immanentist religion just as Hitler produced his version of what he called "a positive relation between Christianity and the new manifestation of the Reich". Our version is decent, democratic and moral in comparison; but they both belong to the same category of religions that have their roots in the immanent urges of society for cohesion, and not in the Word of the Eternal God to men in the Body of Christ. Spiritually dangerous forces always fasten on real human problems and on men's best intentions to deal with them.

To repeat in conclusion what I have said many times before, to meet this situation, or to make ourselves or our children ready when it is found that this "societal" religion does not meet the deepest needs of man, two things are necessary. The theology of Grace and the theology of man's natural life must both be recovered without entirely separating them or merging them in one another—that is, without "dividing the substance or confounding the persons", as it were. If the theology of Creation, Grace, Redemption and the Body of Christ is not recovered, Christians will be content to try merely to sweeten the social drift; the Church will become more and more an appendage of social movements, and the tendency to undo the "Christian revolution" will spread. On the other hand, if the theology of man's natural life is not recovered, if Christians renounce all responsibility for nature and history, if they proclaim a purely apocalytic salvation, then society itself will give the natural and temporal order a divine power, and it will find in some form of paganism or unscriptural idealism the faith to inspire its politics.